TWENTY WEEKS TO TRANSFORMATION

WORKBOOK TO ACCOMPANY

LOVE YOURSELF AND BE HEALED: AWAKENING

DR. JANE E. RACKLEY

WWW.DRJANERACKLEY.COM

Printed in the United States of America

23 22 21 20 19 18 17   1 2 3 4 5

1st printing, February 2017

ISBN: 978-0-9987617-0-1

Table of Contents

Introduction

This book is for the adventurous types who enjoy exploring, uncovering, and understanding what we really are here to accomplish. It is for anyone who has ever asked, and tried to find the answer to *why am I here?* Or, *what is the purpose of my life?* If you have ever asked yourself these questions-congratulate yourself, as these are the first steps toward initiating the *active pursuit* of our own Spiritual Journey. Wouldn't it be fantastic if each day we were able to move throughout our day having a greater understanding of the world we are living within? How would our lives look different if we had the understanding *and* tools to be able to create *major* transformations in our life?

This workbook paired up with the book *Love Yourself And Be Healed: Awakening,* is designed to assist you in creating spiritual transformations in every area of your life. It is simply not enough to read a great spiritual book which may be inspiring, and then not really have a plan to implement the new teachings into your life. This *Transformational Workbook* gives you the step-by-step strategy to take everything within the book, and systematically apply it into your everyday life.

You will find that you will wish to use these books together again and again. Since our lives are dynamic and continually changing with various relationships and events, it is important to periodically re-evaluate all that is occurring. As our awareness and growth increases, so will the variety of different situations in our life. It is only through the *regular* use of every tool we have available which will allow us to experience the breakthroughs to create every possible transformation in our life.

How to Use This Workbook

This workbook follows the same pattern of chapters as *Love Yourself And Be Healed: Awakening.* It gives specific exercises intended to enhance your understanding of the teachings, as well as for use in your day-to-day life. The goal is to help you gradually move further along each day to a higher degree of spiritual *Awakening.*

This may be studied in a group book-study setting, or individually. I suggest the following as an ideal pace the first time through: complete *one chapter each week* for chapters 1-4 for the first four weeks, then *every two weeks* chapters 5-12. The total time to complete the workbook is twenty weeks. The second and subsequent times that the workbook is studied may be condensed as is described in the outline in the *Afterword* at the end of the workbook. Since our lives rapidly change and give us new opportunities for greater lessons, it is important that we continue to actively keep "doing the work" in our lives.

General Workbook Format

Reading Assignment: The sections and applicable page numbers of the book which should be read prior to beginning the next readings and exercises in the workbook.

Summary and Anecdotes of Reading: This section will provide a brief summary or additional narratives designed to assist you in understanding the material.

Key Concepts: This area outlines, defines, and explains any important core ideas.

Exercise: A variety of different types of practical assignments which are designed to assist you in applying the information in your life.

Homework: These are specific assignments which are to be started and either in-progress or completed before beginning the next section. Each of these may be a certain spiritual practice or other action which may be very fundamental, or more advanced depending upon the level of the student.

Buddy Call: Here is outlined the suggested topics to share and review with your *buddy* on your call.

It is important to study the workbook in its intended sequence. Since each chapter builds and introduces concepts systematically, it is important to study and practice the material without skipping anything.

As you begin this *Transformational Workbook,* be sure to really pay attention to everything which starts entering your life. This is the equivalent of you saying *yes,* I am ready to really move more towards my *Awakening.* As you open this door wide, many new lessons, opportunities, ideas, and people will begin to show up in your life. Each of them will have its own message or lesson for you. Be sure to pay attention. If things have been stagnant in your life for some time, you may see things that point you into a whole different direction. Make sure that you notice your dreams at night, as these may come to give you insights or information you never considered as well. You may find it valuable to keep a journal or notebook of the "aha moments" or insights you receive as you continue on your journey. I have learned to always keep a pad of paper on my nightstand. Often in the middle of the night, or early morning those ideas, dreams, or inspirations may come and I will get up even for 5-10 minutes to scribble it down before it gets forgotten.

Finally, remember that there is no *right* or *wrong* way. We each are at our own place in our Spiritual Journey, and that is always the perfect place. The important thing is simply for us to take action in our lives, and then to *keep moving.* So let's get going!

1

It's Time to Wake Up!

Reading Assignment: Read chapter 1 pages 1-11 including, *What is That Something Which is Missing?*

The Buddy Plan

Over thirty years ago when I was on the first day of my Army Basic Training, our Drill Sergeant assigned each of us in our platoon a "buddy." We were each paired up with one other soldier in our platoon. It was explained that through the next eight weeks each *buddy* partner was responsible for keeping in contact, and knowing what was going on with the other person. If our buddy was assigned KP (kitchen police), went on sick call, or was not in our platoon during training for any other reason, we were responsible for knowing what she was doing.

I recall that besides the obvious, *knowing what the other was doing*, it was good to occasionally check-in with another person. Both of us had just been placed into definitely the most difficult and stressful training up until that time we either had experienced. It was helpful that every couple of days we might check-in with each other. It may only have been a rushed, "Are you doing okay?" But just taking even a minute or two of acknowledgment and listening to another person who you know is going through the same stress as you can be quite a relief.

Even though my buddy and I both finished Basic Training and were shipped off to separate corners of the world, we both maintained contact with each other for over twenty years. Every couple of years we would reconnect and check-in to see how the other was doing, and listen to what was new in each other's life.

As we have always heard, there is strength in numbers. Whenever we create a new relationship, there is opportunity for greater learning. If we can find a spiritual-minded person to *buddy* up with as a partner, this allows us to have a greater level of accountability and potential growth. The purpose of having a *buddy* is to help us keep on track with our progress in *doing the work*. Not only does it encourage us to keep the commitments we make to others, but also to ourself. We also have someone who we can routinely contact and practice our listening skills, as well as sharing our own experiences.

Choose Your Buddy

If you are studying this as part of a spiritual book-study group, at this time pair up with another person from your group. If you are studying this as an individual, try to find someone from your spiritual community who may wish to pair up with you to study these books at the same time. If you simply can't find anyone, you will still greatly benefit regardless. However, having a spiritual *buddy* is highly recommended.

It is important to choose someone whom you *do not* already have a close relationship. It is important to avoid choosing for your *buddy* anyone who is: your significant other, family member, close friend, co-worker, or anyone who your life overlaps theirs in any significant way. The best person to choose is usually someone from your Spiritual Community who you may know, yet lead a completely separate life situation.

After choosing your Spiritual *buddy,* take a couple of minutes to exchange information and determine a time in which you both may speak to each other uninterrupted on the phone. You should plan to conduct these phone-meetings each week for the first four weeks, and every two weeks thereafter until finishing the workbook. Plan for each phone-meeting to take *no greater than 30 minutes.* It is important to allow each *buddy* 15 minutes to share from the exercises and realizations during the previous time-period. It is important to *stay on task* and make this time of sharing productive and useful for each person. Yet you want to be sure to honor the time constraints of keeping the meetings no longer than 30 minutes.

My Spiritual Buddy

Summary and Anecdotes of Reading

That one elusive *something* which countless people grasp often in all of the wrong places throughout their whole life, is simply to *awaken*. Yet there are still many who may state, "Why do I need to *awaken* and what purpose would that serve?" There are quite a few who might argue, "But I am happy; I have a good job and a great family. I even grew up in a church where I learned everything I need to know. I have good values, and I follow all of the rules. *Sometimes* I still attend church and think of my beliefs at times. I think this *should* be plenty!" The problem with this way of thinking is this is all we have ever been taught that we should strive for in this life. Many people have been led to believe that there is a stopping point in life. Where it is okay to reach out, and then once attaining that seemingly safe *comfort zone*, that is our arriving place. This is the place in which many feel they have accomplished everything they were told was important in life, and can pretty much coast from there forward. This seeming *comfort zone*, is really the place where most all of the possible spiritual growth and journey has come to a rest or may even completely stop.

It is important that we stop and really take a look at our life, and examine it closely at a window of about the previous five years.

Key Concept

What is our *comfort zone*? We may think of it as as a time period during our life in which we simply seem to be coasting. It is during that time that in which most areas of our lives seem to be going smoothly. The only problem with being *comfortable* in life, is that usually during this time there is little spiritual growth.

Of course many people say that they don't really wish to be uncomfortable either. This is understandable, yet often a person will build a lifetime of avoidance in an attempt to stay comfortable. How can we determine whether we are living our life fully-embracing all of the opportunities which come our direction, or are simply going through the daily motions and not really moving?

Exercise

Take a close look at the last five years of your life. Examine each area, answering each question carefully. Fill out the table as best as possible, following each example.

5

List up to two major events/actions which have occurred during the last *five years* in each of the following areas of your life which you feel has caused you to grow.

Career	Family	Spiritual	Partner/Spouse	Friends	Health	Education
Applied for a new position and was passed over.	Had a long and much needed talk with my sister, and put aside old grudges.	Found and became actively involved in a Spiritual community.	Went on a spiritual retreat with my partner.	Discontinued spending time with a friend who seemed to drain my energy.	Took a fall and fractured my elbow.	Completed a new certification course in my career field.

Count up the total number of items you wrote above. If you have less than four items listed, most likely you are hanging out in your *comfort zone*. If you counted 4-9 items, you are definitely moving forward on your Spiritual Journey. If you had 10 or more, it is highly likely that you are on the *fast track*.

Now look at each item you listed from the previous table. Explain below either what lesson, new understanding, or how did the event/action cause you to grow spiritually or otherwise?

Career	Family	Spiritual	Partner/Spouse	Friends	Health	Education
I was able to see a couple of months later that the position was really not in my best interests. It would have lead me off of my purpose.	I was able to really see her side of things, and listen better than the past. I learned that my own stubborness was causing much of our problem, and was able to stop.	I am sharing with a group of like-minded people. This is allowing me to grow through fellowship, meditation groups, and book-studies.	I had greater insights about my partner's needs and experienced greater growth in myself. This allowed me to communicate better with my partner after the program.	I learned to be a little more careful in selecting my friends. I found that it is not helpful to be with others who spend much time caught up in negativity.	I realized that this was a sign that I need to slow down in my life, and it is important to pay attention to my surroundings.	I finished a certification which is aligned with my higher purpose to serve others. I will be able to serve others in a greater capacity due to this new training.

Look at the table you filled in above. Were you able to connect the events/actions in your life with a lesson or spiritual growth? If you found any part of this difficult, do not worry as you will become much better at this by the end of this workbook.

After examining the table above answer the following questions:

During the last five years, which of the seven areas have I had the greatest amount of Spiritual Growth in my life?_____

_____

_____

Which of the areas have I had the least amount of Spiritual Growth in my life?_____

_____

_____

What do I think are the reasons for the greater areas of growth in my life? And what do I think are the reasons for the lesser areas of growth in my life?_____

_____

_____

_____

Have my relationships with *others* improved during the last five years? If yes, describe in what ways?_____

_____

_____

_____

Has my relationship with *myself* improved during the last five years? If yes, describe in what ways?_____

_____

_____

_____

It is important to understand that these above exercises are intended for us to really see where we are *right now* in our life. At this moment, we only are evaluating our past to determine how much we have grown. Remember that there aren't any *right* or *wrong* answers. This simply helps us to begin the process of how to *really* look at our life. Our intention is to move into a place of true understanding. Once we can accomplish this, we can then set the sail on our boat and move into any direction we choose.

Reading Assignment: Read Chapter 1 pages 11-16 including *Truth vs. Belief.*

Core Concept

My Spiritual Teacher explained once how to determine if a concept is founded in truth or not. That which is truth is always *changeless*. That which is a be*lie*f always *changes*. Also, look what is in the center of the word be*lie*f. So that which is rooted in truth is so today, was the same 5000 years ago, and still will be the same in 10,000 years from now. We can also take this teaching to the next step to recognize that truth is also *timeless*. A be*lie*f, on the other hand, might be one thing today, different 200 years ago, and will change again in 500 years from now.

If we simply accept another person or group's opinion as our own, this falls back into the category of be*lie*f. *Everything* which is established in truth, can be *experienced* by us directly. It is only through our *own* personal experience that we have the ability to discern that which is actually a truth. Once we have the direct knowledge, it will never leave us.

So to be able to recognize in our life the difference between something which is a be*lie*f vs. truth, we must take that which we are evaluating through a cascade of questions.

1. Is the idea/concept *changeless*? This means that it always stays the same, and never changes. If the answer is yes, continue to the next question. If the answer is no, then it is a belief.
2. Is the idea/concept *timeless*? This means that it always has been the same 3000 years ago as it is today. It also means that it will still be the same in 3000 years from today. If the answer is yes, continue to the next question. If the answer is no, then it is a belief.
3. Is it possible for a person to *experience* first-hand the idea/concept? If the answer is yes, continue to the next question. If the answer is no, then it is a belief.
4. Is there any situation or *outside influence* which could alter the idea/concept? If the answer is yes, then it is a belief. If the answer is no, then it is a truth.

Exercise

Select *three* different concepts/ideas from science, spirituality, religion, health, or philosophy. Take each item step-by-step through the above cascade of questions to determine whether it is a be*lie*f or truth. Enter your answers in the table below.

Idea/Concept	The continents sit on plates which are moveable and allow the land of our planet to move. It is named plate techtonics.	It is impossible for a human being to live over the age of 120 years.	The essence, or soul of each person is eternal, having no beginning or ending.			
Is it changeless?	no	no	Yes			
Is it timeless?	no	no	Yes			
Can it be experienced?	yes	yes	Yes			
Can it be influenced?	yes	yes	No			
Is it a belief or truth?	belief	belief	Truth			

Describe how being able to determine the difference between a be*lie*f and *truth* might be valuable in evaluating ideas/concepts of your health, spirituality, religion, philosophy, and science. _____

_____

_____

_____

Take one of the be*lie*fs that you listed above in your table, and state if you feel that most people in society tend to embrace this concept/idea?_____

_____

Do you feel that this be*lie*f is overall beneficial for the people in our society, or do you feel it is detrimental, and in what way?_____

_____

_____

Do you envision that this be*lie*f will eventually change in our society, and if so what do you think it will take to cause it to shift?_____

_____

_____

_____

_____

Homework

Obtain a notebook to keep during your day and near your bed at night. Begin paying attention to any dreams, or insights that you may start to notice throughout your day. Often times these may come in a flash of instant awareness, or even messages from other people. Start writing them down in your journal.

Buddy Call

Take turns with your buddy sharing two events/actions you listed from your first exercise and share what lesson/growth you were able to realize from each of them. Choose one item you listed in your be*lie*f/truth table to share with your partner. Take that item step-by-step through the cascade of four questions, and share how you determined the answer to each question. Then describe whether you determined that it was a be*lief* or truth. Finally, take a minute to share if you each have noticed any new insights, or had any *aha moments* during this week.

2

What is Awakening?

Reading Assignment: Read all of chapter 2 pages 17-23.

Key Concepts

The dictionary definition of *awakening* is: The act of starting to understand something or feel something. The root of the word is *to awaken,* which means: rouse from sleep; cause to stop sleeping. Simply by looking at this definition we might deduce that the opposite of being in a state of *awakening* would be instead a state of *sleeping.* Another way to describe this also is the level, or degree of *awareness* we have in our life. This defined is: the knowledge or perception of a situation or fact. So as we have already established, there are people going through life at all different levels of *awareness*. And this is directly related to the degree in which a person is *awake.* There are many who discuss and describe the term *enlightenment.* This is similar to the concept of *higher awareness. Enlightenment* has been utilized for many centuries to describe the level of spiritual awareness which may be obtained. This has been demonstrated by various Spiritual Masters throughout time. For our purposes, *full enlightenment* may be described as a *constant state* of higher awareness.

Exercise

Explain and describe the differences between *awakening* and *enlightenment.*_____

_____

_____

_____

_____

_____

What do you feel is the importance of *awakening*? _____

_____

_____

_____

_____

What do you feel is the importance of *enlightenment*?_____

_____

_____

_____

_____

Exercise

Look back at your two tables from your exercise on page 6 and 7 in chapter 1 and choose *two* events/actions you listed. Fill in the below table with your two original events/actions again. Think about what other areas of your life such as career, family, spiritual, spouse/partner, friends, health, and education you have noticed that these actions/events have affected. Describe how these other areas have been affected. Finally, describe in what way *today* each of these same areas of your life seem to have shifted, or have been altered by this action/event.

Took a fall and fractured my elbow. I realized that this was a sign that I need to slow down in my life, and it is important to pay attention to my surroundings.		
This also affected my career as I had to slow down, and had to get help with many of my activities at work. It influenced my family life as I was unable to perform several regular household and outdoor chores. I had to get help from others to perform certain tasks. My spiritual life was influenced because I could see that I had created the situation by being critical of other people in similar situations.		
Today I am more cautious to recognize that our bodies need to be nurtured and protected. I know that there are times when it is okay to get help from family and co-workers when it is needed. I have learned that because I was judgemental towards someone else who had a similar injury, that I seemed to draw this experience into my life. This experience helped me to see first-hand the importance of having greater compassion for others, and also allowing others to give me the same.		

Do you feel that each of your chosen actions/events above has allowed you to experience a greater level of *awakening* today than when the original event/action occurred? If yes, explain how much time needed to pass until you were able to understand the significance of these events in your life. Also, describe if there were other events in your life which helped you to be able to see these realizations. If so, what were they?_____

_____

_____

_____

_____

Do you feel that be*lie*fs and truth have a role in either speeding up or slowing down our ability for *awakening* in our life*?* Explain why it is that you feel this way._____

_____

_____

_____

_____

.Homework

Continue to pay attention to any dreams you may have or insights during your day. Keep writing these in your notebook. Then examine them to see if any of these might be related to any of the seven areas of past events/actions which previously occurred in your life. Look to see if you notice any new information which may help you to understand the reasoning for these past events. Also look to see if it may help you to understand any current situation in your life.

Buddy Call

Take turns sharing with your spiritual buddy your understanding of the differences of *awakening* and *enlightenment*. Discuss what the level of importance these each have had for you during your life. Choose one of the events/actions from your exercise above and share what you wrote in the table. Take a minute to share with your buddy any new insights or realizations you have had during this week as a result of completing the workbook exercises or from continuing your notebook.

3

Establishing The Framework

Reading Assignment: Read Chapter 3 pages 24-31 including the sections *The East Teaches the West* and *And Justice For Us All.*

Key Concepts

Throughout the years I have come to understand *Karma* to be that which truly is the equalizer. It is really that which makes the playing field for everyone truly level. *Karma* is simply the law of cause and effect. Everything that we *think, feel, speak* and *act* upon has a creative energy which we may call the *cause*. And the degree or quality of the energetic level which is behind the thoughts, words, feelings and actions are that which determines the eventual outcome, or *effect*.

Exercise

Think about all of the various events which have occurred in your life relating to your family, career, spiritual community, friends, health, school or otherwise within the last *month*. Choose one event or incident which occurred that you are able to recognize that you thought, spoke, felt or acted upon and seemed to trigger one or more other subsequent similar energetic events afterwards. What was the initial event or incident? What other incidents did you notice that day or a within a few days afterwards?_____

_____

_____

_____

_____

_____

_____

Did this initial event and the others which followed seem to have similar feelings? Describe your feelings with each of them (Example- love, joy, peace, happiness, upset, anger, pain, frustration, fear, sadness, etc.)_____

_____

_____

_____

Key Concept

When the student is ready, the teacher will appear. Often throughout our lives there are different times in which to reach the next level of growth, a teacher will become available to us. The teachers who come to us in our lives do so because of our previous words, thoughts, feelings, and actions. We have attracted this person into our life. This is in itself is an event of *Karma,* or the law of *cause* and *effect.*

There are all types of important teachers who we may draw into our lives. A teacher may come to us in the form of a person, in a traditional setting or a non-traditional setting. Our teacher may come to us in the form of a professor, instructor, spiritual teacher, health-care provider, family pet, small child, book, series of books, and any variety of other means. Our teacher may be in our life for a short time, perhaps even for a one-time incident or for a longer period of time.

Our teachers may appear to us in any area of our life. The lessons we learn from them may cross over and benefit us in multiple areas of our lives. We might even look back years later, and recognize the important lesson we needed to learn.

Exercise

Look at each of the major areas of your life and choose three teachers as described above who you recognize helped you to grow in your life. Name the teacher. Then describe at least one or two lessons you were able to learn from that teacher.

Other	Family	Spiritual	Career	Friends	Health	Education	Other
My first pet as a child which was a cat named Julie.							
Once I accidentally allowed her to get out of our house. She ran away and under a low trailer where we couldn't get her out. It was cold and she stayed there for at least three days. One day she ran back into the house. I learned the importance of my own responsibility, and the level of love and desire of family of all living beings.							

Choose two of the teachers you described in the table above. Look at the lesson(s) that you learned from each of them. Describe how what you learned from each of these two teachers have affected your life today. Describe thea areas of your life which there has there been growth as a direct or indirect result?_____

_____

_____

_____

_____

_____

Identify and fill in the table below any teachers you are able to recognize in your life *today*. Who or what are they? Do you have teachers you can identify who are helping you to grow in multiple areas of your life? If one teacher is helping you in multiple areas, name the teacher in each area. Describe what lessons you think they may be in your life to teach you.

Family	Friends	Spiritual	Career	Education	Health	Other

Look at your table above of all of the teachers you currently see in your life. Do they seem similar or different? In what way? Can you identify any kind of link or pattern of the lessons you are currently working on in your life? What is it?_____

_____

_____

_____

_____

Are there some ways for you to better work *with* the teacher(s) you currently see in your life? Name at least one *action* that you can take in your life which you are not doing presently, which would help you to work with one of your teachers better._____

_____

_____

_____

_____

Reading Assignment: Finish reading Chapter 3 pages 32-40 including the sections *Let's Play It Again,* and *Where's The Proof?*

Key Concept

Reincarnation defined by the dictionary is: that an individual has a rebirth into another body after death. This concept has been readily accepted as the truth for centuries throughout many portions of the East. Yet this concept has seemingly eluded many of those in the Western portion of the world.

Another aspect of this which goes hand-in hand is that we are *eternal* in our nature. This means that we have no beginning or end to that energetic substance which makes up our core being. We might also describe ourselves as *timeless.* This is how we might be better able to understand the concept of having multiple lifetimes here on earth or elsewhere.

Exercise

Think about a time during your life in which you went to a place or location for the first time, and had a feeling like you had been there before. Describe what happened and how you felt there. How did it seem familiar to you? Did you notice any triggered feelings or unusual memories while you were there? What were they?_____

_____

_____

_____

_____

_____

Think about a time when you first met someone in your past and noticed that it seemed like you knew the person before. Maybe you noticed that you simply *clicked* and were able to talk with them as though you had known them for a long time. Describe what happened and how you felt during this first interaction. Did you continue to maintain contact with this person? If so, what is the relationship like today?_____

_____

_____

_____

_____

Have you ever noticed a time that you first met a person and had an immediate strong adverse reaction towards them? Perhaps you simply felt that you *didn't like* this person, and yet had no recognizable grounds to base this feeling upon. Describe what happened and how you felt. Did you continue to maintain contact with this person? If so, what is this relationship like today?_____

_____

_____

_____

_____

Have you ever noticed either as a child or adult that you have a particular talent that just came very easily for you? Maybe there is an area that you seemed to need very little instruction, and you were simply able to learn to do easily. It might be drawing, art, writing, reading, building, singing, mechanics, playing a musical instrument, growing plants, or a myriad of other things. What were you able to learn easily? Describe what lead you to discover it? Did it simply feel like you already knew how to do the activitie(s), and were simply being reminded? Are these activitie(s) still a part of your life? If so in what way?_____

_____

_____

_____

_____

Have you ever had a dream during your life which seemed to realistically detail another possible lifetime? What was it? Did it seem very convincing and familiar? Were you able to see any kind of parallel situations which were occurring during your life at that time similar to now? What did you notice?_____

_____

_____

_____

_____

Are there certain types of furniture, clothing, cars, homes, music or other styles that you seem to feel drawn toward which are from a certain era of the past? What are they?_____

_____

_____

_____

_____

_____

_____

Look at each of your answers above to these questions. Do any of these give cause for you to see the suggestion of reincarnation? Look at each one of these and describe how you feel this has impacted your life today. Are you able to spot any possible pattern(s)? If so, what do you notice?_____

_____

_____

_____

_____

_____

_____

Homework

Continue keeping your notebook. Write down any dreams you have during this time. Look to see if you can see any direct or indirect messages which may be related to these exercises. Pay close attention to any particular *flashes* of insight you may notice regarding any lessons you may be currently working on in your life. Write them down. Think about how these may be affecting your life right now. Look at your exercise of the one *action* that you listed which will assist you to work better with one of your current teachers. During this week take this *action*.

Buddy Call

Take turns sharing with your buddy the one event you chose on the exercise during this chapter and all that you noticed that seemed to occur afterwards. Describe whether you felt that you were *in the flow* during the time or *out of the flow*.

Choose your one main teacher you feel is currently helping you the most in your life. Describe to your partner how you feel this teacher is helping you in your life presently.

Describe to your buddy any *aha* moments and what they were that you noticed as you answered the last questions on reincarnation. Finally, share with each other the one *action* you took to help you work better with one of your teachers.

4

The Glue That Unites Us

Reading Assignment: Read all of Chapter 4 pages 41-56.

Key Concept

Many people throughout the years have often been taught that *sticks and stones may break my bones, but words will never hurt me*. However, today we know that this simply isn't correct. Today even science is able to better demonstrate that not simply our actions, but all of our thoughts, words, and feelings affect us and others.

We also have been taught that we should compartmentalize these into good or bad, right or wrong, positive or negative, and so forth. When we are encouraged to categorize everything in this way, we tend to become judgemental. This tends to create more duality among people or even an *us* vs. *them* mindset.

Exercise

Other than the example below, name at least one duality that you have noticed either in your life or society. Do either you or others have a tendency to take one of the two sides and disagree with the others? In what way? (Ex: Democratic Party and Republican Party. Yes, often people will take one or the other side and disagree with the others. There are a multitude of ways in which one party feels the other is wrong and tends to take opposing positions on many issues. These include health care, the national budget, abortion, gay rights, foreign policy, the war(s), education, and more.)_____

_____

_____

Look at the duality you selected above. What do you feel is the best way for people to resolve their differences, and to move to a place of unification in the future?_____

_____

_____

_____

_____

_____

Key Concept

This newer paradigm is simply that everything is *energy*. The dictionary defines energy as: a fundamental entity of nature that is transferred between parts of a system in the production of physical change within the system, and usually regarded as the capacity for doing work. *Energy* is that invisible *stuff* that science at times can measure, but most of the times cannot. It is found in everything, everywhere and is essentially the responsible catalyst for all we can see and that which we cannot.

Dr. Hawkins through his newer research was able to categorize energies into two categories. He found that words, thoughts, feelings, and actions could be categorized into *lower fear-based* energies and *higher love-based* energies. His research showed that energies which are *fear-based* create weakness in the body and those which are *love-based* create strength.

We also are able to distinguish that the higher love-based frequencies tend to create a feeling of expansion and openness in our life. Whereas fear-based frequencies typically cause a feeling of contraction and separation from others.

Exercise

Do you feel that it is important for us to learn to distinguish in our life when we are demonstrating *love-based* energies versus *fear-based* energies? Why is this important?_____

_____

_____

_____

_____

_____

We know that our emotions and feelings directly distinguish whether our state of being is in tune with love-energies or fear-energies. Love-based feelings include love, joy, peace, reason, acceptance, enlightenment, courage, and bliss. Think about all of the activities which have occurred during the last 5-7 days. Choose one activity or event that you are able to distinguish was clearly in alignment with these love-based energies. Describe what happened._____

_____

_____

_____

_____

_____

Describe some of the feelings you experienced during this activity and afterwards._____

_____

_____

_____

_____

Fear-based feelings include fear, pride, anger, desire, shame, grief, apathy, and guilt. Again think about all of the activities which have occurred during the last 5-7 days. Choose one activity or event that you are able to distinguish was clearly in alignment with these fear-based energies. Describe what happened._____

_____

_____

_____

_____

_____

Describe some of the feelings you experienced during this activity and afterwards._____

_____

_____

_____

_____

_____

Look at both of these situations and discuss in what way you feel each situation affected the rest of your activities throughout the day afterwards. Did you notice an increase or decrease in your productivity? Did you notice greater or lesser communication with other people? Was there an improvement or detriment to your overall creativity or the development of new ideas? Did you feel more focused or less focused? Did you feel that you had a greater level of empowerment in your life or less?_____

_____

_____

_____

_____

_____

_____

_____

_____

Look at all of your answers and descriptions above for this exercise. Do you feel that it might be beneficial for you to recognize whether your state of being is aligned with the love-based energies or fear-based energies? Explain how this would better serve you._____

_____

_____

_____

_____

Homework

Start noticing your activities and events throughout your day. Are you able to determine whether you are in a *love-based* or *fear-based* state of being? Write these down in your notebook and distinguish whether your feelings and reactions were aligned with love or fear. Look at the activities which you identified as love-based. For each of these answer the same questions listed in the exercise at the top of this page. Write in your notebook any new realizations or 'aha' moments you may have experienced as a result of doing this work.

Buddy Call

Take turns sharing with your buddy the *love-based* and *fear-based* examples you chose to examine during this chapter. Describe the feelings you noticed and how they affected you. Go through the questions listed for this exercise for each of your situations and discuss what you discovered. Share the one greatest benefit that you feel understanding this concept will bring into your life.

5

Elevating Our Love Experience

Reading Assignment: Read pages 57- 64 including the sections *Feeding the tree of love* and *Just a heartbeat away*.

Key Concept

There are four major areas or components we must focus upon developing in our life when we choose to actively pursue *Awakening* in our life. Similarly, a chair requires four legs to be fully functional and supportive of a person. If one or more of them are missing it will no longer completely perform as a chair. Likewise, if we ignore one or more of these areas we can expect much less advancement on our spiritual journey.

The four essentials are *Love, Power, Discipline* and *Wisdom*. Each of these are inter-connected with each other and have its own unique dynamics. The most expansive area to first understand is *Love*.

There are *three keys* to fully understand and practice to shift into a *love-based* life. The *first* is that we need to fully understand is there are the two energies that each person every day spends feeding. We are either making trips to water the *love* tree or the *fear* tree. *Secondly*, we must learn to develop what is called *discernment*. This means: *the ability to see and understand people, things, or situations clearly and intelligently*. This also is when we are able to perceive subtle, and sometimes not so subtle differences and distinctions in our daily activities. Even when we fully understand about these energies, it can be difficult to *discern* whether we are watering the *love* or *fear* tree. When we are in the middle of some sort of conflict or situation, it can be tough to recognize our own feelings. The best way for us to determine this is to ask ourselves if the way in which we are responding allows us to feel comfortable, light, and uplifted? If this is so, then most likely we are on the *love* side. However, if we notice our experience has feelings of heaviness, discomfort, or in any way irritation, then we are most likely watering the tree of *fear*. *Lastly*, in the cases where we determine that we are handling certain circumstances in our life from a place of *fear*, it is best to fully recognize how we are feeling.

Exercise

Think about each different area of your life including family, spouse/partner, friends, spiritual, career, education, health or any other area. Focus upon the one area which you have noticed the greatest amount of difficulties for you during the last month. This most likely will involve your relationship with another person in one of these. Identify the #1 relationship that you most notice your tendency to go water the *fear-tree* the most frequently. Describe what incidents/events happened._____

_____

_____

_____

Have similar incidents happened previously? If so, briefly describe these. What is the length of time ago when you first noticed this difficulty first began?_____

_____

_____

_____

_____

_____

Describe some of the feelings you can identify during this most recent difficult incident. During and immediately after the incident were there certain areas of your body that you could feel any discomfort? If so, what did you notice and where?_____

_____

_____

_____

_____

_____

Use your *discernment* and look for any potential patterns that you may identify looking at the interactions during the history of this difficulty. Describe any that you may see._____

_____

_____

_____

_____

Think back to this incident. Did you realize at the time that you were watering the *fear-plant*?____

_____

If not, how long did it take you to first *discern* this after this incident?_____

_____

Key Concept

Sai Maa teaches that the heart energetically has two components, or compartments. The first of which is the center of *human love*. This is the energetic love in which many people mistaken through life for *love*. Actually, this is of a lower vibration than *love* in its purer form. This *human love* is usually *conditional*. This is demonstrated when a person sends out the feeling *I love this (person or thing) because s(he)/it gives me (something) in return*. The person with this type of love will send only what one be*lie*ves to be love, thinking that most likely one will get something in return.

The second compartment of the heart houses *divine love*. This is the energetic love which carries the highest vibration. This type of love is *unconditional*. Divine love is demonstrated *when the person loves someone or something, simply for the sake of loving*. One does not expect to receive *anything* in return, and the love is ever-present regardless of the situation or actions involved.

Exercise

Give an example that you have experienced in one of your own relationships that demonstrates the concept of *divine love*. Describe what happened._____

_____

_____

_____

_____

_____

Describe how the definition of *divine love* applies to this specific occurance._____

_____

_____

_____

_____

Give an example that you have experienced in one of your own relationships that demonstrates the concept of *human love*. Describe what happened._____

_____

_____

_____

_____

_____

Describe how the definition of *human love* applies to this specific occurance._____

_____

_____

_____

_____

Use your *discernment* to now examine your #1 difficult relationship you identified in the previous exercise. Look at everything which occurred in this most recent incident. Are you able to *discern* whether either you or the other person(s) involved were demonstrating either *human love* or *divine love* towards the other person(s). If so, which one? Explain how the action meets the definition described above._____

_____

_____

_____

_____

Reading Assignment: Read pages 64-75 including the sections *Taming the beast within, Practicing in the trenches,* and *Is love in the air?*

Tool For Transformation

It is good that we have practiced using our *discernment* to better identify any situations in our life which are blocking us from being in a state of *divine love.* Now that we have learned how to detect these, it is time to learn how to transform these lower energies into into higher vibrations. This is the practice which we may use over and over again to help shift anything which we may identify as *fear-based* in our life over into the higher state of *divine love.*

1. Identify a situation that you wish to transform through using your *discernment.* Choose any situation or relationship in which you are able to recognize that you are feeding the tree of *fear.*

2. Find a quiet place to sit and identify any feelings you may notice as you think about the situation. Allow yourself to fully acknowledge and face the feeling or emotions you may be experiencing. These may include anger, jealousy, worry, blame, anxiety, regret, guilt, fear or shame.

3. Continue to allow yourself to think about the situation and let the feelings to arise within you. Permit yourself to fully be in whatever emotions that may come. If tears come don't fight them back. Allow them to wash over you. Allow between 2-3 minutes for yourself to fully face these feelings. You will most likely begin to feel discomfort in the umbilicus area near the *belly button.*

4. Now take your hands and place them both face up with the palm of one hand touching the bottom of the other. Position both of your hands *cupped together* like this against the front of your body, and just under the location of your *belly button.* Both palms should still be facing up creating a scoop with your hands. Now slowly move your hands straight up the front of your body, imagining that you are moving those lower energies up until your hands are just in front of your *heart-center.* This is where the sternum, or breastbone is located. *Now* slowly move your cupped hands up and over *scooping* the energies directly into your *heart-center.* Your hands are now both palms forward touching your body directly over the middle of your heart.

5. *Finally,* continue to sit and remain silent for a couple of minutes, keeping your hands touching your *heart-center.* Whenever you feel ready, gently open your eyes.

You will most likely notice an immediate shift in yourself. If you attempt to think about the situation again, you will notice there has been a change. There will be a difference in the way you now perceive the situation. You will notice how it has lost its grasp on you. *Any* lower energy cannot continue when it is moved to the *heart-center* where there is *divine love.* This is yet another life-altering teaching by Sai Maa.

Exercise

Look at the #1 relationship difficulty you selected and described in the exercise earlier. Read through the *Tool for transformation* above. Using this situation and this tool perform each of the five steps above. After completing the steps identify and describe below any shift or changes you may have noticed. These may be very noticable or subtle._____

_____

_____

_____

Day #2: Using your new 5-step transformational tool above repeat this again. Use the *same* difficult situation you used for the previous day. After completing the steps identify and describe below any shift or changes you may have noticed. These may be very noticable or subtle.-

_____

_____

_____

_____

Day #3: Using your new 5-step transformational tool above repeat this again. Use the *same* difficult situation you used for the previous day. After completing the steps identify and describe below any shift or changes you may have noticed. These may be very noticable or subtle.-

_____

_____

_____

_____

Day #4: Using your new 5-step transformational tool above repeat this again. Use the *same* difficult situation you used for the previous day. After completing the steps identify and describe below any shift or changes you may have noticed. These may be very noticable or subtle.-

_____

_____

_____

_____

_____

Day #5: Using your new 5-step transformational tool above repeat this again. Use the *same* difficult situation you used for the previous day. After completing the steps identify and describe below any shift or changes you may have noticed. These may be very noticable or subtle.-

_____

_____

_____

_____

Day #6: Using your new 5-step transformational tool above repeat this again. Use the *same* difficult situation you used for the previous day. After completing the steps identify and describe below any shift or changes you may have noticed. These may be very noticable or subtle.-

_____

_____

_____

_____

Day #7: Using your new 5-step transformational tool above repeat this again. Use the *same* difficult situation you used for the previous day. After completing the steps identify and describe below any shift or changes you may have noticed. These may be very noticable or subtle.-

_____

_____

_____

_____

After you have used your new transformational tool each day for *seven* days or have performed this a total of *seven* different total sessions; look at the dynamics of the overall situation or relationship you selected. Are you able to notice *any* changes in the situation or relationship? If so, what differences have you noticed? Does it seem like your own level of reactivity has lessened? Describe any changes you have noticed in the other individual(s) involved._____

_____

_____

_____

_____

_____

_____

Make a commitment to continue to use this tool to help transform this situation. If you notice that a shift has occurred, but there is still more work left to accomplish- plan to perform another 3-4 more sessions each week until you feel that there has been a noticable change. After this it may only be necessary to perform additional sessions as may be needed.

After you feel that this situation has become more resolved, you may choose another situation you wish to bring these higher energies for transformation. It is also important to remember that any relationship or situation which has had a great amount of *fear* continuously throughout a longer period of time may take awhile to completely transform. It may be in these situations that you see smaller incremental improvements. Nevertheless, always recognize that there is always a lesson for us to learn during such a conflict. Oftentimes as a result of using this tool one may suddenly realize *what is its root cause*. Be open to any of these potential *aha* moments you may experience using this tool.

Reading Assignment: Read pages 75-92 including the sections *Interlocking components of divine love, Living without conditions,* and O*ur furry friends are the wayshowers.*

Key Concepts

Divine love is again completely *unconditional* and *pure* in nature and can be expressed to ourselves or towards others. We can better comprehend how to practice this in our day to day lives, by moving it from being so idealistic and esoteric and breaking it down into its interlocking major components. We may think of each of these as a strand which is braided amongst the others as though we are creating a really strong rope. If each of these are present, we can expect to have the strongest tensile-strength rope. If any are absent or weak, we can expect that our rope will not hold our weight nearly as well. If we choose to develop the optimal level of *divine love* in our lives, it is important that we fully understand each of these interlocking strands in our rope.

Interlocking Components of Divine Love

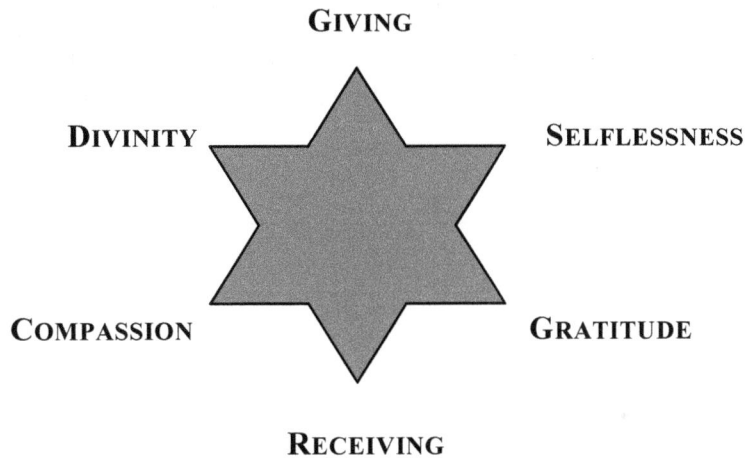

GIVING

DIVINITY

SELFLESSNESS

COMPASSION

GRATITUDE

RECEIVING

The first of these components we will examine is *selflessness*. *Selflessness* is exactly as it seems, it is when we are focusing upon other people's needs. It is when we think about our self less.

Exercise

Choose one of your family pets and describe an incident that you witnessed in which your pet displayed *selflessness*. What happened? Describe any of the traits that you noticed your pet displayed during the incident._____

_____

_____

_____

_____

Think about an incident in which you witnessed a person such as a child or adult display *selflessness* to another. This may be an incident in which you were involved or not. What happened? Describe any of the traits that you noticed this person display during the incident.___

_____

_____

_____

Take a moment to examine these two different incidents you described above demonstrating *selflessness*. Look and see if you may notice any similarities. How are they similar? In what way? Are any of the traits the same in both of the situations you described, if so, which are the same?_____

_____

_____

_____

_____

Look at both of these situations and list below at least *four* of the major traits that *you feel* are most important for a person to display *selflessness* towards others.(ie: affection, understanding, generosity, etc)_____

_____

Look at the list you created above. How often do you notice that you display these four characteristics towards others during your day-to-day life? Name one way in which you feel you might be able to increase these characteristics within yourself._____

_____

_____

_____

_____

Now take the four traits that you listed above and create your own affirmation below using an I am statement for each of them.(Example: if your characteristic is affection, the affirmation may become: *I am affectionate towards others.*)

1._____

2._____

3._____

4._____

Now re-write the four affirmations you have created on two different notecards and place one of them on the front of your refrigerator and the other on your bathroom mirror. Keep these in place for at least the next couple of weeks. Every time you go to the refrigerator visualize, say or think each of your affirmations. While you are brushing your teeth each morning visualize and think each of your affirmations. It is important to not simply state, visualize or think these in a lackluster manner. Rather using higher-level feelings of enthusiasm and passion will allow these to eventually gain a greater foot-hold in your life. Upon completing this for at least one week describe anything which you have noticed that seems to have shifted in this area for you._____

_____

_____

_____

_____

_____

_____

Homework

Write in your notebook after using your first transformational tool on your #1 difficult relationship for a few days any important insights that you may notice. During this time start to notice if any new ideas may begin to flow in your direction. Or see if you start having insights or solutions which seem to *come to you* about the situation that you are working upon. Pay attention to these and write them down. Ask yourself *how might I begin to implement this right now in my life*? If you are able to *discern* any actions that you might be able to take to help the situation, make a plan and take the needed action.

Buddy Call

Take turns sharing with your buddy the example of *divine love* and *human love* you described earlier in this chapter and how each of these fit the outlined definitions. Take turns briefly describing to your partner the #1 difficult relationship you selected to use your new 5-step tool of transformation. Share with each other any possible shifts you have begun to notice during this practice. Share the four traits you decided were the most important characteristics of a person who demonstrates *selflessness*. Take turns reading the four affirmations you created. Then discuss any changes you may have noticed during your week since you have been imagining, stating, and thinking these. Take a minute each to describe any one greatest insight or *aha moment* that you may have received performing this work during the last couple of weeks.

6

Regain Compassion and Giving

Reading Assignment: Read pages 93-106 including the sections *We can do small things with great love,* and *First day on the street.*

Key Concept

The next characteristic, which is a component of divine love is *compassion*. The definition of *compassion* is: the sympathetic *consciousness* of other's distress together with the desire to alleviate it. If we break down the word compassion further into its two components, there is the prefix *com-* and the word *passion*. The prefix com- means *with* or *together*. The word *passion* is: a strong feeling of enthusiasm or excitement for doing something or about something. *Compassion* is witnessing or experiencing something in another living being, and having a great desire to take action to assist. This is divine love in its pure essence.

Exercise

We may practice compassion in a wide variety of smaller and larger ways. There are opportunities within our families, with friends, our spiritual communities, our career, the community, and with strangers. Examine each of these areas in you life and describe two separate acts of *compassion* you recall that you displayed towards another person during the last couple of weeks. These may be smaller or larger. (Example: took some homemade soup to a friend who was sick in his home, helped someone in the parking lot of the grocery store pick up a bag of dropped groceries, spent the afternoon at the nursing home visiting a family member, or volunteered to help one of your co-workers get caught up with charting her paperwork.)_____

_____

_____

_____

_____

Now look at these same areas of your life. Can you think of any situation within your family, career, spiritual community, friends or community that might need an act of compassion? It could be that you notice someone presently struggling in some way who maybe could use some type of additional assistance. Describe any situation that comes to mind below._____

_____

_____

_____

_____

Now look at each situation you wrote above. Is there anything you could do which might help this person? What is it? Make a plan to take action._____

_____

_____

_____

_____

Name one way you feel that you may be able to become more *compassionate* towards other people._____

_____

_____

_____

Write below the affirmation: *I am compassionate towards other people.* Then obtain two notecards and write the affirmation on each of them. Place one at the top of your other notecard on your refrigerator and bathroom mirror, just above your other notecard on *selflessness. Imagine, state* and *think* this affirmation each time you go into the refrigerator and also while you are brushing your teeth each day. _____

_____

_____

Reading Assignment: Read pages 106-113 including the sections *Heart-centered giving* and *Having the time of your life.*

Key Concept

The next key component of Divine Love is *giving. Giving* is closely related to *compassion* and *selflessness*, yet needs its own category.

A minister of the Unity New Thought Spiritual Movement, Rev. Stretton Smith, developed a program called the 4T prosperity program in 1988. This program, and it's teachings have become widely embraced throughout the Unity Movement. The core concept of Rev. Smith's program is that we need to give to others our time, talents, treasures, and tithes. This action of giving will in turn tend to manifest a greater level of abundance in our life. Although our major reason for giving to others is not simply to receive back abundance in our life, it certainly can become a side-benefit. Looking at the 4 T's, *time, talents, treasures* and *tithing*, are an excellent way to fully examine all of the ways we may give to others.

The first way we might give of ourself is our *time.* Where am I giving my *time* to others? The second is we may give of our *talents.* How do I give to others through the use of my *talents*? Otherwise, how do I use my own unique abilities to help serve others? Third, we may give our *treasures.* This is giving of money, or our financial wealth or other possessions to others. How do I give my *treasures* to benefit others? Lastly, we may give our *tithes.* This is financially helping to support the organization which spiritually feeds us. How do I financially support my spiritual home or community?

In the ancient language of *sanskrit* the word *seva* means *selfless service.* This represents *giving* of ourselves simply for the sake of giving. This is when we give our *time* to others as *selfless service.*

Exercise:

First look at the area of *giving* your *time* to others. Examine each major area in your life including your family, friends, career, spiritual community, and other community. Identify and list the activities below in which you *give* your time.(Examples: babysit the grandchildren, help to clean the spiritual community, lead a bookstudy group or volunteering at the local food bank)

_____

_____

_____

_____

_____

On the table below estimate the approximate total number of hours each **month** that you are giving your *time* in each different category.

	Career	Family	Friends	Spiritual Community	Regular Community
Total Monthly Hours Example 1	160 hrs.	25 hrs.	5 hrs.	24 hrs.	0 hrs.
Your Total Monthly Hours					

Now add up your total hours in all of the categories above and divide the total number of hours by four. In our example this would be 160+25+5+24= 214. Then 214/4= 53.5. Look at your end number. This number indicates your total *time* in which you are *giving* to others during your week. If we assume that most of us require about 8 hours of sleep each night, this gives the average person about 112 hours each week of time we have available for our conscious life. Although there is certainly no set rule or formula, if we divide these 112 hours into half we have 56 hours. If we look at our average hours of service to others and it is below 56 hours, it is likely that we are at a pretty good balance. This example of 53.5 hours it is easy to recognize that this person is balanced in the amount of *time* given to others. The other 58.5 hours of this person's week would be used for normal activities of daily living *and* more importantly *giving time* to oneself. If we calculate our number and find it is 60 or greater hours each week, this may indicate that we are *giving* too much of our *time* towards others and not enough for ourself. If we calculate our number and find that it is 40 or less hours each week, this may indicate that we are *giving* too little of our *time* towards others.

Perform your calculations below to determine your average weekly *time* of giving to *others.*

_____

_____

_____

During a typical week, do you mostly feel energized and seem to be able to accomplish most that you choose each week? Or do you at times feel like you don't have enough energy to accomplish all of your commitments each week?_____

_____

_____

_____

If you answered that you feel your energy seems lower and you often do not have the energy to accomplish your commitments each week, examine where and how you are using your *time* to serve others. Is there an area which seems to be unbalanced? Which area? Do you feel that *decreasing* your number of commitments would help to lower this feeling of depleted energy? Or does it seem that during your typical week you do not spend enough *time* serving others? Or do you feel that *increasing* your number of commitments would help to increase your overall energy?_____

_____

_____

_____

If you answered that you feel your energy seems high throughout the typical week, still look at each of the major areas you analyzed your total *time.* Is there any area which seems to be unbalanced? If so, which area?_____

_____

_____

Now look at all of your answers. Do you feel that you are balanced in the amount of *time* you are serving others each week? Or do you feel that you are *giving* too much *time* during a typical week? Or do you feel that you are *giving* too little *time* to others during a typical week? If you feel there is a lack of balance write down one thing you can either decrease or increase from your *time* serving others. Take the action to make this change in your life._____

_____

_____

_____

_____

If you determined that your typical week is unbalanced and you need to *decrease* your *time* serving others, write one thing that you can do to *increase* your *time* serving yourself. Take the action to make this change in your life._____

_____

_____

_____

Reading Assignment: Read pages 113-139 including the section *Our gifts to the world, The parable of the talents, The bulb is still burning, If you get into a ditch don't keep digging,* and *Turning points are always pivotal.*

Key Concept

The next of the important T's which are a component of giving are our *talents.* A talent is: A special ability that allows someone to do something well.

Exercise

There are a myriad of ways in which we may express our special *talents* in our lifes. Our special gifts and talents might involve that which we do in our career or any other area of our life. Our talents may include a wide array of aspects of our life. Examples may include mechanical ability, baking cakes and cookies, singing and playing piano, growing vegetables and plants, taking photographs of children, leading other people, computer programing, teaching others, painting pictures, repairing appliances, driving large trucks, writing poetry, and riding a bicycle in the mountains.

Look at each major area of your life and list *at least* 1-3 *talents* or abilities that you feel that you do well in each category. Make sure that you write down a *minimum* of *at least six* of your total talents below.

Home	Career	Hobbies	Family	Community	Other
I grow a large vegetable garden and grow plants well. I can landscape the yard well.	I work well with other people. I am a good speaker in front of groups. I am great at initiating new projects that the company needs and following through with them.	I have read many historical biographies and know a lot about the history of the U.S.	I am tutoring my child in math and his grades have improved greatly. I organize the family vacations and we take at least two really fun trips a year.	I help lead and organize other volunteers at the local food bank.	

Exercise

Now think about any activity that you feel a great amount of joy and love while you are doing it. This is usually something that you can easily get *lost in the moment* and lose all track of time. These are the activities in your life that *light you up* while you are doing them. List below at *least* your top *seven* activities that you love to do the most.

1_____

2_____

3_____

4 _____

5 _____

6 _____

7 _____

8 _____

9 _____

10 _____

Exercise

Now compare the list above of your favorite activities with the previous list of your *talents* and abilities. Are any of the activities the same or related? List below all of the activities from the two lists that are the same or closely related.

1 _____

2 _____

3 _____

4 _____

5 _____

6 _____

7 _____

8 _____

9 _____

What does this tell you? Do you feel that there is a correlation between our *talents* and the things we most love to do? Explain how you feel._____

_____

_____

_____

_____

Now count up the total number of *talents* you described in the first table. This helps to indicate how much you are using your own *talent* in all aspects of your life. If you scored 10 or more, it is most likely that you are utilizing your talents in your life pretty well. If you scored 7-9, it is likely that you are utilizing your talents in your life, but there may be room for more improvement. If you scored 6 or less, it is likely that you are not utilizing your talents in your life as well as possible. Write down your score below. Now look again at your list of *favorite activities* for any which **did not** correlate to your list of talents. Write each of them down below._

_____

_____

_____

_____

_____

_____

_____

Now look at this list of your *favorite activities*. Why are these not part of my life? How can I bring these more into my life?_____

_____

_____

_____

_____

Exercise

If your score was greater than an eight, choose *one* of your *favorite activities* you listed on the previous page and make a plan to begin to incorporate this into your life. If your score was less than an eight, choose *one* from your list and make a plan to move this activity into your life, and after two weeks, choose *one more* from your list and make a plan to move this activity into your life as well. Write below the steps you took, and what you noticed happen after integrating each activity into your life.

Activity 1_____

_____

_____

_____

_____

_____

_____

Activity 2_____

_____

_____

_____

_____

Key Concept

Looking at the four T's of giving: *treasures* and *tithes* really seem to overlap and are fairly similar. Both *treasures* and *tithes* are usually represented by money, but could also be other gifts which we may give of ourself which have either a financial or non-financial value. The difference of these two are simply determined by *which* organization or person it is who are receiving our gifts. If the organization or person *is not* one in which spiritually feeds us personally, then the gifts we give to these are our *treasures.* If the gifts we give to an organization *is* one in which spiritually feeds us personally, then the gifts we give to these are called *tithes.* When we look at these two areas, it is these which have a key connection to the level of financial abundance in our life. Not only do these two impact our ability to fully give of ourself to others, but they influence us directly on what is available for us to receive.

Many have called this concept *the law of circulation,* and we have called it the law of *karma,* or law of *cause and effect.* This area is no different than any other in our life. Everything which we send out in our life, including our gifts of *treasures* and *tithes* carry a creative energy, and its level of energetic vibration will come back to us.

Exercise

Take a look at your life during the last *one year* and list below into each different category any *treasure* which you have given to others. Some examples of giving our *treasures* might include: donating canned goods to the local food pantry, giving money to a charity that supports Native American children, giving our old computer to the local school, having money removed from each paycheck to go to a couple of United Way charities, taking a Thanksgiving meal to a family in need on the holiday, and giving short-term financial support to a family member who is struggling.

Family	Career	Community	Other

Take a look at your life during the last one year and list below any *tithes* which you have given to your spiritual community or other spiritual organization. Remember that this should be only the community or organization which spiritually feeds you. Some examples of giving our tithes might include: giving a regular financial donation to the spiritual center or church in which you attend, donating two truck-loads of dirt to help repave the parking lot at your spiritual center or church, donating several items for your spiritual center's annual yard sale, and donating financially to a non-profit organization which provides you and others spiritual books and information.

Spiritual Community	Other

Now look at the table you filled in previously. Do you feel that you are giving enough of your *treasures* to others?_____

Now look at the table just above. Do you feel that you are giving enough of your *tithes* to the organizations which spiritually feed you?_____

Now look at both tables. Does it look like the *treasures* and *tithes* you have given during the last year are fairly balanced? If not, which of the two seems to be greater?_____

Now look at your overall personal finances during the last year. Do you feel that your financial flow during this time has been mostly easy? Has the last year for you been mostly financial abundant? Or has there been some financial difficulties?_____

_____

_____

Now look at your overall level of financial abundance during the last year and compare this to the level of *giving* your *treasures* and *tithes* during the last year. Do you feel that there is a relationship between these? Explain the relationship._____

_____

_____

_____

If you noticed that you have had some financial difficulties during the last year , do you correlate this to a lower level of giving of your *treasures* and *tithes?* If this is the case, choose at least one thing you may do to increase your *giving* of *treasures* or *tithes.* Take the needed action. Describe your chosen plan._____

_____

_____

_____

_____

_____

_____

Write below the affirmation: *I am giving fully to myself and others.* Then obtain two notecards and write the affirmation on each of them. Place one at the top of your other notecard on your refrigerator and bathroom mirror, just above your other notecard on *compassion. Imagine, state* and *think* this affirmation each time you go into the refrigerator and also while you are brushing your teeth each day. _____

_____

Homework

Examine each of your exercise assignments which required you to take certain steps and action. Write in your notebook any required steps you need to take to complete each of them. Continue to pay attention to any new insights that you notice during these two weeks and write them in your notebook.

Buddy Call

Take turns sharing with your buddy if there is a situation in your life right now that you could demonstrate more *compassion*. Describe what did you do to help with this situation? Share with your partner what you determined is your average hours each week of *giving*. Share some things you discovered about your *giving* of your *time* and how you determined if you currently give too much, too little or about the right amount. Describe any actions you took and why. Share what you discovered about yourself after completing the exercise on *talents*. What actions did you take? What did you learn after examining your *treasures* and *tithes* during the past year? Did you decide to make changes? Take a minute each to describe any one greatest insight or *aha moment* that you may have received performing this work during the last couple of weeks.

7

To Thine Own Self Love

Reading Assignment: Read pages 140-143 including the section *what goes around.*

Key Concept

There are many people grounded in all various religious and spiritual groups who have been taught the importance of *giving*. However, seemingly there are very few who have been taught that *receiving* is equally as important as giving. Yet *receiving* is one of the six important components of *divine love*. When this is completely absent in a person's life, it is very easy for the person to eventually become greatly unbalanced.

Many of us are taught in the West that we are to think of others first and not of ourselves. Also many of us are raised to be*lieve* that it is *always* better to *give* rather than to *receive*. However, what this seems to develop in most people, is a sense that all *giving* is good and all *receiving* is bad. The truth of the matter is that while *giving* is a good thing, *receiving* is also just as good, and best when there is an equal balance of these two in our lives.

Exercise

Think about the last *3 months* in every area of your life including your career, family, spiritual community, community, friends or other areas. Make a list of everything small or large that you can remember in which you have *received* from others. Be sure to **exclude** any *receiving* during meditation as this will be discussed later. (Examples might include: your boss gave you a compliment, your grandchild gave you a hug and said *I love you,* a friend gave you an extra copy of a spiritual book to read, some of your friends came and helped you move, or someone at the grocery store helped you pick up several canned goods you accidentally knocked off the shelf.) List below as many as you can remember below.

1 _____

2 _____

3 _____

4 _____

5 _____

6 _____

7 _____

8 _____

9 _____

10 _____

11 _____

12 _____

Now count up the total number of incidents of *receiving* you listed above. If you were able to recall at least 10 or more incidents during the last 3 months, you are probably well-balanced in allowing others to *give* to you. If you counted 7-9 this might be an area in which you need to examine closer within yourself, and determine if you need to open yourself up more to *receiving*. If you counted 6 or fewer above, this indicates that *receiving* is an area in your life which may be unbalanced and may need more of your focus and attention.

Now look at each of the incidents individually you listed above. Examine each of these closely and describe below how you felt as you *received* from each of these other people. Did you feel open and accepting from others? Or did you feel uncomfortable in any way? If so, in what way?

1 _____

2 _____

3 _____

4_____

5_____

6_____

7_____

8_____

9_____

10_____

11_____

12_____

Now look at what you wrote above. Did you find that you mostly felt comfortable in allowing others to *give* to you? Or did you discover that you felt uncomfortable? Explain why this might be important in determining your ability to *receive* from others._____

_____

_____

_____

_____

_____

Now look back onto the previous lesson at the exercise where you listed the different activities in which you *give* your *time* to others. Describe below the overall feelings that you have whenever you are engaged in *giving* to others during these activities.

_____

_____

_____

_____

_____

Examine your feelings above when you are actively *giving* to others. Does it seem to make you feel more expanded and open? What does this imply about the importance of actively practicing *receiving* in our life? When we allow ourselves to *receive* from others, are we allowing others to experience *giving* in their life? What is its importance to us and others?

_____

_____

_____

_____

_____

Write below the affirmation: *I am receiving easily from the universe and others.* Then obtain two notecards and write the affirmation on each of them. Place one at the top of your other notecard on your refrigerator and bathroom mirror, just above your notecard on *giving.* *Imagine, state* and *think* this affirmation each time you go into the refrigerator and also while you are brushing your teeth each day. _____

_____

_____

Reading Assignment: Read pages 143-158 including the sections *The Greatest Secret Revealed, Do You Go To The Bathroom?, Use Your Imagination, Sanskrit Mantras, English Mantras/Affirmations, Remembering Ourself and Others,* and *What Is So Great?*

Key Concept

Meditation has been practiced since the beginning of time in all of the most advanced civilizations. Most every sacred historical text either indirectly or directly refers to meditation. Recently, there have been numerous scientific studies which verify the many benefits *received* through the practice of regular meditation.

Present day science is verifying that which has been known since the beginning of time. The practice of meditation is the greatest vehicle for humanity to *receive* all that we are *aware* of that is possible, and all of which we are *unaware* is possible. Meditation is the gateway which every person no matter where one lives, age, social status, religion, financial position, regardless of *anything*, all have equal access.

The regular practice of meditation is the key which allows us to not only develop a physiologically balanced and healthy body, but to access everything. Meditation allows us to find the solution to any issue. It allows us to experience first-hand that we are truly connected to everything. During meditation we witness through our own awareness that which cannot be described in words, and simply know. This is the means to our growth in awareness in every aspect of our being and life. It is here that we encounter the essence of our own reality. We do so by entering into the place of stillness, where there is nothing and everything all in one.

Exercise

If you are new to meditation, decide on a particular location in your home which is quiet and you won't be interrupted. Select a chair that you can use exclusively as your own *meditation chair*. Place it in this location of your home. Ideally this should be the corner of a secluded room such as your bedroom or other room where you will not be disturbed. You will wish to obtain any cushions or pillows to make your meditation chair comfortable.

Although it is not a requirement to have one, you may wish to find a small end table to create your own *puja table.* You may place pictures of any Spiritual Masters you choose, candles, incense, special crystals or other meaningful items which you feel will help you remember and connect to your own divinity. It is important if you do choose to create a *puja table* that you include a photo of yourself on your table. This is to serve as a reminder that *you* are divine just the same as any of the Masters, and you are to be honored just the same.

Exercise

Look at your daily schedule. If you currently do not practice meditation during the morning, what time do you normally wake up? If you are new to meditation and currently do not practice daily in the morning, set your alarm to wake up 20 minutes earlier than usual. If you currently practice meditation each day in the morning, go to the next exercise. Make a commitment to do this *daily.* If you are concerned about losing 20 minutes of sleep, the benefits you will *receive* will far outweigh the sleep.

Exercise

Commit to practicing this *breathing meditation* every day for *seven* days. If you are new to meditation start out practicing for five minutes. Once this seems easier, then you may gradually wish to increase your time. It is important to sit comfortably with the spine erect. The feet should be flat on the floor and hands may rest comfortable with open palms up on each of your thighs. Initially, we want to focus our attention on our breath. During this breathing meditation, use the breath through the nostrils only and not through the mouth. Close your outer eyes, and take a deep breath in and *imagine* that above your head there is a large light in which you are connected. Then *imagine* seeing a tube of light running into the top of your head, and coursing throughout the whole spinal cord towards the bottom of the feet and into the earth. As you take an *in* breath, imagine that you are drawing that light above through the tube into the body and down into the ground. Then as you begin to exhale slowly, imagine the breath is pushing this light back up from the feet through the body and through the head and above again. *Imagine* this cord of light which you are attached, as a bright dazzling golden color. Continue to slowly and rhythmically draw a breath *in* seeing the light from the breath coursing into the cord of light and increasing its intensity. Then slowly release the breath *out* continuing to watch the pattern of light moving throughout the body. Slowly continue this same pattern of breathwork. Continue focusing upon your breath rhythmically in this way until you feel you wish to stop and simply be silent. Then allow yourself to become silent. This may last only a few seconds at first or perhaps not at all in the beginning. This is okay. The important thing is that there is *no* right or wrong way to practice this. Every person's experience is unique. Don't worry about thoughts which may come, simply continue to focus upon your breath. Start out practicing this meditation for about 5 minutes. Then gradually you may begin to naturally increase the time as you become more comfortable with the practice.

Exercise

After you have practiced the *breathing meditation* for at least five days write down what you have experienced below. Has the practice each day seemed to get easier for you? Describe any other changes you have noticed since beginning this practice._____

_____

_____

_____

_____

_____

_____

_____

_____

Exercise

The next common practice of meditation is through the use of *affirmations* or *mantras*. These are specific, usually short phrases or words which may be spoken, chanted or even simply thought. These may be used in your own native language, or possibly in Sanskrit. Look at the following list of Sanskrit and English mantras and *choose two* that you feel most drawn towards.

I am Love –*Invocation of love.*

I am Peace –*Invocation of peace.*

I am Joy –*Invocation of joy.*

I am that I am –*I am divinity(God) presence that I am within.*

Om –*The primordial sound of the universe.*

Om Namah Shivaya –*I honor the divine consciousness of Shiva*

Om Shanti Shanti Shanti – *Invocation of peace*

Plan to use these same two mantras for your meditation consistently. It is important to not change your mantras or to add any additional mantras until these have been well practiced. Remember that during meditation with the use of *mantras,* each has a unique energy which you are sending out. As you send these specific vibrational energies out during your meditation, the same quality of frequencies will return to you. The mantra helps you to stay focused and *tuned in* to *receive* and be open to all that you may experience during your meditation. Using a mantra is similar to walking on a path that you know leads to the ocean which is full of everything. Maybe the first time you walk the path it seems a little strange and awkward, and as you practice more you will start to know the trail and it becomes easier. Eventually, you can find your way to the ocean easily on that path. Only after much consistent practice should you add another mantra or change either of them.

Exercise

After you have practiced your *breathing meditation* each morning for seven days, now commit to practicing *mantra meditation* for the next seven days. Use the first *mantra* you have chosen. Similar to *breathing meditation* close your outer eyes, sit with your spine erect and take in a deep in-breath through the nostrils, and slowly exhale simultaneously chanting or speaking your affirmation/mantra slowly during the out breath. The full affirmation/mantra should be completed by the end of the outbreath. Next, take a deep breath in again through the nostrils, and slowly exhale again repeating the mantra. Continue until you have performed repeating your mantra three times. After finishing your mantra allow yourself to sit still in silence for a minute or two.

Next, use the second *mantra* you selected and repeat the procedure same as above.

After three days of practicing using three breaths with your *mantra meditation,* increase the number of times you repeat *each* of your mantras to 16. It is helpful to use a *mala* or prayer beads to help you to keep count if you have one. However, it is not necessary to have one. I have found that it is just as easy to use your fingers. Your hands should be relaxed and open on each of your thighs during meditation. You may easily keep count by touching your thumb to each of your four fingers sequentially on your right hand, then in the same way to each of the four fingers on your left hand, then repeat with your right and then left hand once again. Touching four fingers on the right, four on left, four on right, and then four on the left allows you to keep count to 16.

Exercise

After you have practiced the *mantra meditation* for at least *five* days write down what you have experienced below. Has the practice each day seemed to get easier for you? Describe any other changes you have noticed since beginning this practice._____

_____

_____

_____

_____

_____

_____

_____

_____

Exercise

I recommend that you practice your two basic mantras/affirmations during meditations consistently during your daily meditations for at least a couple of months before adding any new or different ones to your practice. Years ago it was unusual for a Spiritual Master to give a student *one mantra* to use in daily meditation practice for many months and perhaps up to a few years before allowing the student to begin practice with a different mantra.

It is important to know how to select and create your own mantra when you are ready. I have found that a mantra that you personally have chosen, and created for yourself will be much more powerful and meaningful.

First of all, decide which one attribute you choose to bring more into your life. It may be after performing many of the exercises in this workbook that you recognize that it would be beneficial if you attracted greater health. It could be that you notice that you need to become more compassionate towards others. Or perhaps you choose to serve others in a greater capacity as a teacher. I feel when using mantras during meditation that always one of the mantras must be one which will focus upon our own divinity. Then any additional mantras may be one that we choose to bring more of a certain thing into our lives. During our meditation I feel it is best to use these other types of mantras/affirmations first, and at the end use our mantra of divinity. The mantras of divinity include , but are not limited to such mantras as: Om, Om Namah Shivaya, I am that I am, and The Gayatri Mantra. These each are ancient mantras which have been used for centuries by all of The Masters and allow us to reconnect ourselves most directly.

There are two major points to remember in creating your own mantra. Keep it as simple as possible, and always keep it in the present tense by using the words *I am*.

Here's a great example to use and one you want to avoid:

Avoid: I am wanting to live a life of great health.(This is too passive and wordy.)

Instead: I am living a life of great health.(This is short, more powerful and fully in the present)

For a mantra during meditation you may wish to shorten your mantra as much as possible. So in this case you may wish to make your mantra shorter: *I am healthy*. Or: *I am great health*.

Choose two aspects that you wish to have expressed more into your life. Create your own affirmations or mantras below. After a couple of months practicing your *mantra meditation* with your *original* two mantras, either add one or both of your newly created mantras into your meditation practice. At this point you may feel free during your meditation to practice either two or three mantras. However, it is important during one any one meditation session to practice no greater than three mantras during your meditation.

_____

_____

_____

_____

Exercise

Write below your two new affirmations/mantras again. Then obtain two notecards and write both affirmations on each of them. Place one at the top of your other notecards on your refrigerator and bathroom mirror, just above your notecard on *receiving*. *Imagine, state* and *think* this affirmation each time you go into the refrigerator and also while you are brushing your teeth each day._____

_____

_____

_____

Reading Assignment: Read pages 159-160 including the section *Remembering Ourself and Others*.

Key Concept

The next major component of Divine Love is *Divinity*. This realization may be experienced through the practice of meditation. *Divinity* is: the state of realizing one's self is directly from God.

This is the key component of *Divine love* which so many people have faltered away, or have yet to know. It is the recognition that *every* single person on this planet is of a pure, *Divine* essence. Each are connected to one another, and equally connected to the *One Divine Source* most call *God.* Also, it is the concept that we are not only connected with this Divine essence, but are also one and the same.

Exercise

There is no one simple method which will instantly demonstrate this concept of our own *Divinity* to anyone. This is a concept which can *only* become understood through the practice and experience of meditation. Once again, the key is continued practice. Then most often when you least expect it, you will have your own unique encounter which will allow you to experience and *know* first-hand that this is correct.

However, there is one demonstration which my Spiritual Teacher, Sai Maa, has used throughout the years to help us to experience that our core essence is light. Towards the end of your meditation practice in a session, continue to keep your eyes closed. Start by accelerating your breath. Take a deep breath in keeping your mouth shut and inhaling quickly and deeply through your nostrils, and then quickly push your breath back out through your nose. Keep doing this quickly. This is called *pranayama breathing* and has been used for centuries. When performing this correctly and quickly enough, you should feel your diaphram moving quickly with each breath. Your quick breaths should sound like a locomotive getting revved up. Continue with your quick breaths drawing in and out through your nose gradually becoming faster and faster. Continue to perform this as fast as you can, rythmically for a total of at least 4-5 minutes. (If you are performing this fast enough and properly, the last couple of minutes of this practice will feel uncomfortable) If you wear glasses be sure to remove them first before beginning this practice. Then stop the breaths and very quickly, and take your first two fingers on each hand keeping your eyes closed, at first gently press your fingers onto both of your eyelids. Now gradually press your fingers a little harder onto your eyes, keeping them there for about 30 seconds. After about 30 seconds take your fingers off of your eyes. You may continue to sit in silence a couple of more minutes until you finish your meditation. After you finish your meditation describe what you saw and experienced below when you pressed your fingers on your eyes. What does this demonstrate to us about ourselves?_____

_____

_____

_____

Reading Assignment: Read pages 160-174 including the sections *What Is So Great?. Stop Focusing on the Ditch,* and *Green Eggs and Ham.*

Core Concept

The final component of *divine love* is *gratitude.* Gratitude is: the state of feeling or showing thanks or appreciation for the benefits received in life.

Gratitude is very similar to looking at the age-old question, *which came first, the chicken or the egg?* When we look at *divine love* and *gratitude*, it is the same conundrum. We know that these two energies are intertwined intimately together. It is simply not possible for one of these to completely stand-alone without the other.

As we grow up we are mostly taught at first to acknowledge *things* which we are given, or that which are our *possessions,* and to be thankful for these items.

However, there is another whole realm of practicing *gratitude* which often is overlooked in our lives. There is also all of which occurs to us throughout our life, which are the *tangible* and *intangible* benefits we may receive from the *events* and *circumstances* in our life. This concept moves us more into the esoteric domain of the practice of gratitude. This is the area many have difficulty understanding and fully embracing. Yet it is a crucial area, which if we fully grasp the dynamics will enhance our greatest growth.

Each day in our lives we experience a chain of these events and circumstances. There are those that we mostly welcome and enjoy, as well as others that may be unpleasant to a greater or lesser degree. It is our perception and *reactions* to these, which determines whether we are living a life filled with plenty of gratitude, or are not.

Exercise

Take a look at the two trees below. One of them depicts what our *tree of complaints* and our *tree of gratitude* might look like. You will notice that one looks more healthy and strong while the other one looks weaker and the branches look more crooked. It is obvious that the more frequently we visit our *tree of gratitude* and feed it, then this tree will grow strong roots in our life and become one of our greatest assets. However, if we are feeding our *tree of complaints* more frequently, then likewise this will be what grows the strongest in our lives and overshadow the higher energy state of gratitude. Which of the two trees below is your *tree of gratitude* and which of them is your *tree of complaints?* How might we determine which one we are watering the most in our life?

For this exercise you will need two empty same-size cups, a large blank piece of paper, a pen, scissors and tape. Cut a strip of paper and write on the label *My Tree of Gratitude* and tape it onto your first cup. Then do the same with your second cup labeling it *My Tree of Complaints.* Then cut the rest of your paper into several strips approximately ¾ of an inch wide and about 4-5 inches in length. Keep these together somewhere prominent that you will notice them each day such as on your dining room table. During the next three days at the end of the evening sit down just before you go to bed and take an inventory of all that occurred through your day. First think about every time that you either spoke, thought, took action or had a feeling of gratitude. Take a slip of paper and for each one write down: *I was grateful today for*(fill in the action, thought, feelings or words you expressed of thankfulness including what it was for). Then after you finish writing each one down on your paper, fold them each up and put them into your cup labeled *My Tree of Gratitude.* Next, do the same procedure and think of each time this day that you either spoke, thought, took action or had a feeling of complaint. Similarly write each one down on a separate slip of paper: *I complained today about* (fill in the action, thought, feelings or words you expressed of complaint including what it was about) Fold each one up and put them into your cup labeled *My Tree of Complaints.* Continue this procedure each night for three days.

Which Of These Is Your *Tree Of Gratitude?*

After three days dump out each of the cups and tally up how many slips were in your *Tree of Gratitude* and *Tree of Complaints.* Open each of them and first lay out your papers which list all of your *gratitudes.* Next lay out all of your papers which list each of your *complaints.* Write down your list of *gratitudes* and *complaints* in the next charts.

Gratitudes:

1 _____
2 _____
3 _____
4 _____
5 _____
6 _____
7 _____
8 _____
9 _____
10 _____
11 _____
12 _____
13 _____
14 _____
15 _____
16 _____

Complaints:

1 _____
2 _____
3 _____
4 _____
5 _____
6 _____
7 _____
8 _____

9_____

10_____

11_____

12_____

13_____

14_____

15_____

16_____

Read each of your *gratitudes* and then write down how you feel after reading these. Read each of your *complaints* and then write down how you feel after reading these. Are you able to see any patterns? If so what? Write down any ways that you think you might be able to bring more gratitude into your life._____

_____

_____

_____

_____

_____

_____

_____

_____

Exercise

Once again there are primarily three areas in which we might experience *gratitude* in our life. The first and easiest to recognize of the three are for *things*. The second and third are not as easy to recognize and are for *events* and *circumstances* in our life. Look at each item you listed in your *gratitude* list and at the right of each listing write down if it is in the category of a *thing, event* or *circumstance*. Next look at your list of *complaints* and at the right of each of these listings write down if it is in the category of a *thing, event* or *circumstance*. Now count up the number in your *gratitude* list that were in each of *things*. Then count up the number in this list that were either *events* and *circumstances*. Were there more that you listed which were *things* or more that were *events* and *circumstances?* If you had a greater number of *events* and *circumstances* than *things,* congratulate yourself as this is a sign that you are recognizing the importance of these in your life. Now look at your list of *complaints* and likewise count up the number of *things* and the number of *events* and *circumstances* combined together. Were there more that you listed which were *events* and *circumstances* or more that were *things?*_____

_____

_____

_____

_____

_____

 It is likely for most people that your *complaints* were more about *events* and *circumstances.* Now look at your list of *complaints* again and look to see how you may turn these thoughts, words, feelings or actions around instead into something that you can feel *gratitude* for in your life. Think about and write down below on each one of your list of *complaints* at least one reason that whatever the *thing, event* or *circumstance* which ocurred in your life may be beneficial for you. Then shift and look at how instead you might feel *gratitude* for this experience in your life as you are able to recognize its benefits for you.

1_____

2_____

3_____

4_____

5_____

6_____

7_____

8_____

9_____

10_____

11_____

12_____

13 _____

14 _____

15 _____

16 _____

Exercise

Write below the affirmation: *I am grateful for everything in my life.* Then obtain two notecards and write the affirmation on each of them. Place one at the top of your other notecards on your refrigerator and bathroom mirror, just above your notecard having your two new *mantras.* *Imagine, state* and *think* these affirmations each time you go into the refrigerator and also while you are brushing your teeth each day._____

_____

_____

_____

Homework

Obtain two large pieces of paper and take all of your notecards which contain all of your affirmations. Write each affirmation on your paper neatly in a manner in which there is still room for you to add an additional 4-5 more affirmations towards the bottom of each paper. Neatly affix your affirmation paper on your bathroom mirror and refrigerator. Continue to *imagine, state* and *think* each of your affirmations each time you go into the refrigerator and also while you are brushing your teeth each day.

Continue to pay attention to any new insights that you notice during these two weeks and write them in your notebook.

Buddy Call

Share with your buddy what you discovered in the *receiving* exercise you performed at the first of this chapter. Did you find that you are as comfortable to *receive* from others as you feel to *give?* Share with your spiritual partner any experiences you noticed after practicing your *breathing meditation* and also your *mantra meditation.* Also share the two *mantras* you created in the exercise to eventually use in a couple of months. Next share with your partner your experience after practicing the *pranayama breathing* and pressing your eyelids. Share what you discovered after tallying up your three days of *gratitudes* vs. *complaints.* Choose at least two of your complaints and explain how you were able to turn these around into feeling gratitude for both of these instead. Share with your partner any major *aha* moment(s) which occurred for you during these past two weeks

8

Wind Beneath My Wings

Reading Assignment: Read pages 175-187 including the sections *Living On The Edge* and *Passion Meets The Pavement.*

Key Concept

Once again, we must examine the four major essentials key to actively pursue our *awakening* journey. We have fully explored all of the major aspects of *Divine Love.* Now we must remember there are yet three other important legs, which are needed to create a strong *chair* to support us as we continue to move forward in *awakening.* The second leg of our chair is *power.* Power is defined as: the ability to act or produce an effect.

It is important for us to always remember that *power is passion;* and *passion is power.* When we recognize that these two are intimately connected, it is much easier to understand how to incorporate this vital element into our life.

Passion is defined as: a strong feeling of enthusiasm or excitement for something, or about doing something. So if we look at power and passion, we can easily see how these are both linked.

We have learned the importance of our *thoughts*, *words*, and *actions* and that these create the reality and conditions in which we live. We must understand that each of these are simply empty shells, merely having inert potential until they become activated. They only become creative in our lives once the emotional component of *feeling* charges them. One of the higher levels of *feeling* we can express which moves these from working *passively*, or not at all, to working as an *active energy* in our life is *Passion.* When we remain focused, excited, and filled with passion about any task continuing with this feeling consistently over time it, will always lead to the expression of greater *Power* in life. If we are able to fully display in our life *passion* in all that we do, it will create a major effect(*power*) in every area of our life.

Exercise

Power and *Passion* are synonymous with each other. Often we don't realize that the greatest successes in every area of our life occurs when we are exhibiting a great level of *passion*. Think back throughout the years of your life in each of the following areas and describe as many of your *major* successes that you remember.

	School	Career	Home	Community	Other
Age 10 - 19					
Age 20 - 29					
Age 30 - 39					
Age 40 - 49					
Age 50 - 59					
Age 60- 69					
Age 70 +					

Now look at each of the successes that you listed above and think back to all of the circumstances surrounding them. Examine each individually and ask yourself: Did I feel *passionate* about this activity during the time in which I was performing it? If the answer is yes, circle it. Now list each success of yours from the table above that you circled below individually.

_____

_____

_____

_____

_____

_____

_____

_____

_____

_____

Now look at each of the successes that you listed above in which you felt *passionate* before or during the activity. On a scale of 1-10, rank what level of *passion* you remember while you were performing this activity. 1= only a little bit and 10= a great amount. Write the *passion ranking* next to each activity above. Afterwards look at each of your successes. Is there a pattern with your rankings? Do your greater successes seem to have a higher *passion ranking* than your smaller successes? What does this indicate to us? Write down your correlations below.

_____

_____

_____

_____

_____

_____

Reading Assignment: Read pages 187-189 including the section *The 20 Percent Principle.*

Key Concept

There is a principle which was first noticed and named the *Pareto Principle* after its proposer Vilfredo Federico Damaso Pareto (1848-1923), a French-born Italian engineer. He observed that where a large number of factors contribute to a result, the majority (about 80 percent) of the result is due to the contributions of a minority (about 20 percent) of the factors.

If we use this same principle to look at our life. When we know that by definition *the majority(about 80 percent) of a result is due to the contributions of a minority(about 20 percent) of the factors.* We can us this same rationalization when we look at our life.

Exercise

Let's look at our life. We shall treat our life as though it is a large organization broken into several different categories. Look at the table you completed previously from page 44. Fill in the total number of hours during a month you determined from this pevious exercise that you spend in each of the activities in the top row. Next, look at each category and determine how many of these hours would you estimate that you are performing activities in which you feel *passion*? Remember that an activity in which we feel passion is when we are enjoying ourself and having fun, or are fully engaged enough that we lose all track of time. Write into the second line how many of the total hours you typically feel that you are fully engaged and are experiencing passion. As an example, maybe you spend 160 hours per month serving in your career. Then think of all of the typical activities you perform during these hours and make an estimate of how many of these hours you are experiencing fun, joy and passion as you perform the activities.

Life Categories	Career	Family (Relationships)	Friends (Relationships)	Spiritual Community	Community (Other)
Total number Monthly Hours From Page 44					
Total Monthly Hours I feel Passion, Fun and Joy					
% of my time I experience Passion, Fun and Joy					

Now look at each of the categories above and in the third block calculate the total percentage of time that you are experiencing Passion, Fun or Joy in each of your major life categories.

Example: you have a total hours/ month in Career is 160 in block 1 and the hours feeling passion in block 2 are 55. So 55/160= 34.3% So in block 3 write 34%. Complete this for each category.

Finally, look at each of your life categories above. Is each category *at least* 20% or greater? If they all are congratulations!! It is most likely that you are living your life with the *Wind Beneath Your Wings* and are enjoying enough passion in your life to keep you soaring to greater new heights. If you notice any area that misses the mark of 20% or greater, circle those area(s). Look at any areas that are less than 20%. If any of the areas are lower, notice which ones and complete the following exercise.

Increasing *Passion* in Career/Family/Friends/Spiritual Community/Community/Other

Take 3-4 minutes and close your eyes and think about every activity you remember between the age of 6 to age 16 that you loved to do. Anything that you remember doing that you simply had lots of fun doing that excited you during this time. Relax and breath into your childhood and remember your most fun and exciting activities. Then open your eyes and quickly write a list with no thinking or judgements of everything that comes to you. No matter how big or small or whether it seems significant or not. Examples might be: I loved to read. I loved making paintings. I loved learning history. I played music. I loved to plant flowers with my Mom. I loved taking things apart and fixing things. I loved babysitting the neighbor kids. I loved playing sports. I loved camping. I loved traveling. I loved cooking and baking. I loved computers, looking at the stars, etc.

_____

_____

_____

_____

_____

_____

_____

_____

_____

Now look at your list above and circle each activity that you *still do today* and is a part of your life. It is highly usual that many of our individual talents and the purpose of our life will show up very early in our life. That which we are passionate and love doing as a child can often times be our guiding light to help us stay on track throughout our life. Did you circle at least 75% or more of the things above that brought you joy as a child? If not, why? Also are at least 2-3 of the items you circled activities you do now as a part of your career? If not, really pay attention to this. How can you bring more of these activities to your career? Now look at each of the items that you *did not* circle and select the top 5 from your list you feel you enjoyed the most and write them below.

1_____

2_____

3_____

4_____

5_____

Next to each item write down which life area you could integrate this activity back into your life. Make sure to focus on integrating activies into any of the life areas which were less than 20% for you above. Then choose 2-3 of these and write a plan below of how you will move these fun activities back into your life. Example: I am volunteering to help teach the children in my Spiritual Community. I am planning to go travel and camp with my family on a trip this spring. I am reading the new xyz book on my profession. Also be sure to include a date when you plan to implement these into your life.

1._____

_____

2._____

_____

3._____

_____

Homework:

At the bottom of your paper of affirmations write :*I am living life with Passion.* Neatly affix your affirmation paper on your bathroom mirror and refrigerator. Continue to *imagine, state* and *think* each of your affirmations each time you go into the refrigerator and also while you are brushing your teeth each day.

Continue to pay attention to any new insights that you notice during these two weeks and write them in your notebook.

Buddy Call:

Take turns sharing with your buddy *three* of your sucesses you noted in your life, and to what degree of *passion* you experienced during this time and its importance. Share briefly the results you noticed in each of your major life areas and if you experience greater than 20% passion in each area. Share what you noticed, and any insights after you brainstormed the activities you loved during your childhood. Did you notice at least 2-3 of them in your current career? Share the 2-3 childhood activities you chose to reintegrate into your life and how you plan to do this. Share the date(s) in which you plan to implement each of the activities with your partner.

9

Wisdom Of The Ages

Reading Assignment: Read pages 190 -197 including the section *Learning To Swim With The River.*

Key Concept

The next essential leg to support our chair is *Wisdom.* This is essential on our journey and is key to our reaching a greater level of mastery. *Wisdom is:* a wise attitude, belief or course of action. *Wise is:* the ability of an individual to have a deep understanding, keen discernment, and a capacity for sound judgement. So as we examine the various events in our life, it becomes important to really practice the ability to separate ourselves from being so caught up into the actual drama of each event. Then our *capacity* to have a deeper understanding, discernment, and sound judgement is increased which allows us to have greater *wisdom.*

Exercise

As we progress through our life, there are a variety of events which occur. Some may seem fairly small and may affect us in smaller ways. Others may be larger and have a greater impact in our lives. It is important for us to learn to practice examining both the larger and smaller events *throughout* our life as each of them have importance. Events may occur in any aspect of a life area such as career, family, friends, spiritual community, community and other areas. List below during the previous *three months* as many *smaller* events you have noticed in your life. Examples: Received a speeding ticket, Tripped and fell and sprained my wrist, I received a 5 year service award at my work, I was asked to be a bride's maid in my friend's wedding, The music director in my spiritual community asked me to perform in a music program. My spouse/partner and I went on a weekend vacation.

1 _____

2 _____

3 _____

4 _____

5 _____

6 _____

7 _____

8 _____

9 _____

10 _____

11 _____

12 _____

At the end of each of your smaller events you listed above, write down on a scale of 1 – 10, 1 being the least possible amount of emotional feeling you noticed during the event and 10 being the greatest amount of emotional feeling you noticed while experiencing the event. Only ascribe the degree in which you felt emotion. Example: Receiving a speeding ticket. If you felt a high level of anxiety and upset write an 8 or 9. Receiving the 5 year service award at work. If you felt neutral and felt it was not a big deal write a 1 or 2.

Next, think about everything during the last *two years,* and write down as many larger events as you noticed in your life. Examples: You were offered a promotion in your job. You became married. You were diagnosed with a health condition in which a surgery was recommended. A loved one made her transition in life. You became a new parent. You moved to a new city and started a new job. You were involved in a car accident. Someone broke into your car and stole it. You were given a prestigious award in your career. Again write down on a scale of 1 – 10, 1 being the least possible amount of emotional feeling you noticed during the event and 10 being the greatest amount of emotional feeling you noticed while experiencing the event. Only ascribe the level you felt emotion.

1 _____

2 _____

3_____

4_____

5_____

6_____

7_____

8_____

9_____

10_____

11_____

12_____

Now look at each of the smaller events you listed above in the first list. How many of these events did you score its emotional effect upon you at a level of a 7 or above?

_____

Look at each of the larger events you listed above in the second list. How many of these events did you score its emotional effect upon you at a level of a 7 or above?

_____

Would you expect the smaller or larger events in your life to carry a greater emotional impact upon you? _____What conclusions can you make from this? _____

_____

_____

Do the smaller events seem to have as great of an emotional impact upon you as the larger events?_____

Reading Assignment: Read pages 197-203 *Learning To Avoid Distraction* and *The Art of Being Wisdom.*

Key Concept

The key elements we need to learn to bring greater *Wisdom* into our life is through increasing *humility,* eliminating *ignorance,* using *discernment,* and identifying and eliminating *distraction.* *Humility* is the quality of being humble. Being humble is not thinking of oneself as being greater or better than another person. This does *not* mean we think of ourselves as *less than* another. Practicing *humility* is when we *actively listen* to others. We may speak less and really listen to others. We recognize the needs of not only ourselves. We allow others to have a voice and acknowledge and allow their contributions for the good of all. *Ignorance* is being uninformed or unaware. It can also mean we do have adequate information and choose to *ignore* the importance of it. *Discernment* is the ability to see and understand people, things, and situations clearly and intelligently. Lastly *Distraction* is: the state or act of being distracted. It is being unable to think about, or pay attention to something.

Exercise

Look at *each* one of the events you wrote above in both of your lists. Make at least one copy of the next page in your workbook to keep to practice this exercise again. This regular practice will assist you to obtain greater wisdom in your life. *Wisdom* only comes eventually with practice. As it is with every journey, there is never an ending place, simply more practice to attain greater wisdom. For *each event* (large and small)answer each question in sequence. Then you may wish later to create a new list *every 3 months* of your most recent large and small events. Then go through this cascade of questions to evaluate each one. Regular practice will allow you to start to gain more insights and mastery over the various situations and events in your life. The goal of this exercise is to have a method to be able to better guide this boat called *your life* through the waters. Rather than the boat moving through the water haphazardly, soon you will find that you are guiding it purposefully. Being able to *identify* when our life is going astray of the direction we have set for ourselves is 90% of the solution. The other 10% required to redirect ourselves becomes easier with time.

Write the event._____

_____

How well did I practice *active listening* with others? _____

What opportunities did I have to listen to others?_____

_____

_____

What could I do differently next time to improve my *active listening?*_____

_____

_____

Was there an opportunity for me to acknowledge the value of another person? Did I acknowledge the person? If not, how can I change it or do it differently next time?_____

_____

_____

Did I fully utilize all of the knowledge available to me in this event? How so?_____

_____

Were there ways I could have utilized the knowledge available to me better? What can I do now or next time to improve the outcome?_____

_____

Did I have any helpful information that I chose to ignor during this event? If so what? How may I improve this next time?_____

_____

Close your eyes and take 2-3 minutes and pretend to be someone else(besides you) watching this event on a movie screen. Open your eyes and write down anything not written above you discern from the people, relationships, etc._____

_____

Does this event seem to keep you in alignment with your purpose in life? Or does it seem like any type of *distraction*? If so, explain what action you choose to take now or next time?

_____

_____

Write the event._____

_____

How well did I practice *active listening* with others? _____

What opportunities did I have to listen to others?_____

_____

_____

What could I do differently next time to improve my *active listening?*_____

_____

_____

Was there an opportunity for me to acknowledge the value of another person? Did I acknowledge the person? If not, how can I change it or do it differently next time?_____

_____

_____

Did I fully utilize all of the knowledge available to me in this event? How so?_____

_____

Were there ways I could have utilized the knowledge available to me better? What can I do now or next time to improve the outcome?_____

_____

Did I have any helpful information that I chose to ignor during this event? If so what? How may I improve this next time?_____

_____

Close your eyes and take 2-3 minutes and pretend to be someone else(besides you) watching this event on a movie screen. Open your eyes and write down anything not written above you discern from the people, relationships, etc._____

_____

Does this event seem to keep you in alignment with your purpose in life? Or does it seem like any type of *distraction*? If so, explain what action you choose to take now or next time?

_____

_____

Write the event._____

_____

How well did I practice *active listening* with others? _____

What opportunities did I have to listen to others?_____

_____

_____

What could I do differently next time to improve my *active listening?*_____

_____

_____

Was there an opportunity for me to acknowledge the value of another person? Did I acknowledge the person? If not, how can I change it or do it differently next time?_____

_____

_____

Did I fully utilize all of the knowledge available to me in this event? How so?_____

_____

Were there ways I could have utilized the knowledge available to me better? What can I do now or next time to improve the outcome?_____

_____

Did I have any helpful information that I chose to ignor during this event? If so what? How may I improve this next time?_____

_____

Close your eyes and take 2-3 minutes and pretend to be someone else(besides you) watching this event on a movie screen. Open your eyes and write down anything not written above you discern from the people, relationships, etc._____

_____

Does this event seem to keep you in alignment with your purpose in life? Or does it seem like any type of *distraction*? If so, explain what action you choose to take now or next time?

_____

_____

Write the event._____

_____

How well did I practice *active listening* with others? _____

What opportunities did I have to listen to others?_____

_____

_____

What could I do differently next time to improve my *active listening?*_____

_____

_____

Was there an opportunity for me to acknowledge the value of another person? Did I acknowledge the person? If not, how can I change it or do it differently next time?_____

_____

_____

Did I fully utilize all of the knowledge available to me in this event? How so?_____

_____

Were there ways I could have utilized the knowledge available to me better? What can I do now or next time to improve the outcome?_____

_____

Did I have any helpful information that I chose to ignor during this event? If so what? How may I improve this next time?_____

_____

Close your eyes and take 2-3 minutes and pretend to be someone else(besides you) watching this event on a movie screen. Open your eyes and write down anything not written above you discern from the people, relationships, etc._____

_____

Does this event seem to keep you in alignment with your purpose in life? Or does it seem like any type of *distraction*? If so, explain what action you choose to take now or next time?

_____

_____

Write the event._____

_____

How well did I practice *active listening* with others? _____

What opportunities did I have to listen to others?_____

_____

_____

What could I do differently next time to improve my *active listening?*_____

_____

_____

Was there an opportunity for me to acknowledge the value of another person? Did I acknowledge the person? If not, how can I change it or do it differently next time?_____

_____

_____

Did I fully utilize all of the knowledge available to me in this event? How so?_____

_____

Were there ways I could have utilized the knowledge available to me better? What can I do now or next time to improve the outcome?_____

_____

Did I have any helpful information that I chose to ignor during this event? If so what? How may I improve this next time?_____

_____

Close your eyes and take 2-3 minutes and pretend to be someone else(besides you) watching this event on a movie screen. Open your eyes and write down anything not written above you discern from the people, relationships, etc._____

_____

Does this event seem to keep you in alignment with your purpose in life? Or does it seem like any type of *distraction*? If so, explain what action you choose to take now or next time?

_____

Write the event._____

_____

How well did I practice *active listening* with others? _____

What opportunities did I have to listen to others?_____

_____

_____

What could I do differently next time to improve my *active listening?*_____

_____

_____

Was there an opportunity for me to acknowledge the value of another person? Did I acknowledge the person? If not, how can I change it or do it differently next time?_____

_____

_____

Did I fully utilize all of the knowledge available to me in this event? How so?_____

_____

Were there ways I could have utilized the knowledge available to me better? What can I do now or next time to improve the outcome?_____

_____

Did I have any helpful information that I chose to ignor during this event? If so what? How may I improve this next time?_____

_____

Close your eyes and take 2-3 minutes and pretend to be someone else(besides you) watching this event on a movie screen. Open your eyes and write down anything not written above you discern from the people, relationships, etc._____

_____

Does this event seem to keep you in alignment with your purpose in life? Or does it seem like any type of *distraction*? If so, explain what action you choose to take now or next time?

_____

_____

Write the event._____

_____

How well did I practice *active listening* with others? _____

What opportunities did I have to listen to others?_____

_____

_____

What could I do differently next time to improve my *active listening?*_____

_____

_____

Was there an opportunity for me to acknowledge the value of another person? Did I acknowledge the person? If not, how can I change it or do it differently next time?_____

_____

_____

Did I fully utilize all of the knowledge available to me in this event? How so?_____

_____

Were there ways I could have utilized the knowledge available to me better? What can I do now or next time to improve the outcome?_____

_____

Did I have any helpful information that I chose to ignor during this event? If so what? How may I improve this next time?_____

_____

Close your eyes and take 2-3 minutes and pretend to be someone else (besides you) watching this event on a movie screen. Open your eyes and write down anything not written above you discern from the people, relationships, etc._____

_____

Does this event seem to keep you in alignment with your purpose in life? Or does it seem like any type of *distraction*? If so, explain what action you choose to take now or next time?

_____

_____

Write the event._____

_____

How well did I practice *active listening* with others? _____

What opportunities did I have to listen to others?_____

_____

_____

What could I do differently next time to improve my *active listening?*_____

_____

_____

Was there an opportunity for me to acknowledge the value of another person? Did I acknowledge the person? If not, how can I change it or do it differently next time?_____

_____

_____

Did I fully utilize all of the knowledge available to me in this event? How so?_____

_____

Were there ways I could have utilized the knowledge available to me better? What can I do now or next time to improve the outcome?_____

_____

Did I have any helpful information that I chose to ignor during this event? If so what? How may I improve this next time?_____

_____

Close your eyes and take 2-3 minutes and pretend to be someone else(besides you) watching this event on a movie screen. Open your eyes and write down anything not written above you discern from the people, relationships, etc._____

_____

Does this event seem to keep you in alignment with your purpose in life? Or does it seem like any type of *distraction*? If so, explain what action you choose to take now or next time?

_____

_____

Write the event._____

_____

How well did I practice *active listening* with others? _____

What opportunities did I have to listen to others?_____

_____

_____

What could I do differently next time to improve my *active listening?*_____

_____

_____

Was there an opportunity for me to acknowledge the value of another person? Did I acknowledge the person? If not, how can I change it or do it differently next time?_____

_____

_____

Did I fully utilize all of the knowledge available to me in this event? How so?_____

_____

Were there ways I could have utilized the knowledge available to me better? What can I do now or next time to improve the outcome?_____

_____

Did I have any helpful information that I chose to ignor during this event? If so what? How may I improve this next time?_____

_____

Close your eyes and take 2-3 minutes and pretend to be someone else(besides you) watching this event on a movie screen. Open your eyes and write down anything not written above you discern from the people, relationships, etc._____

_____

Does this event seem to keep you in alignment with your purpose in life? Or does it seem like any type of *distraction*? If so, explain what action you choose to take now or next time?

_____

_____

Now look at each of the events you worked through above. Are you able to recognize any similarities or patterns? If so, what are they?_____

_____

_____

Choose the *one event* above that seems to feel like it is most influencing your life right now. Just before you begin your meditation in the morning, set an intention to ask your higher self for any guidance you may be needing at this time. Ask the question and set the intention, then simply allow. Pay attention to anything you notice during or after the meditation. Do this for a total of 3 of your meditations. Notice if there are any realizations, messages from other people, intuitions or other insights surrounding this during the next week. Write your discoveries._____

_____

_____

_____

_____

_____

Homework:

At the bottom of your paper of affirmations write: *I am living life with Wisdom.* Neatly affix your affirmation paper on your bathroom mirror and refrigerator. Continue to *imagine, state* and *think* each of your affirmations each time you go into the refrigerator and also while you are brushing your teeth each day.

Continue to pay attention to any new insights that you notice during these two weeks and write them in your notebook.

Buddy Call:

Take turns sharing with your buddy what realizations you discovered after analyzing the degree of emotional impact of smaller events in your life vs. the larger events in your life. Discuss any *aha* moments you had and/or important takeaways from this practice. Select two of your important events, and share your worksheet that you completed on each of them with your partner. Then share whatever patterns you were able to identify. Finally, share with each other anything new you discovered during your meditations during the following week after doing this work.

10

Master's In Discipline

Reading Assignment: Read pages 204-207.

Key Concept:

We finally arrive to our fourth leg of support in our chair. It is important to remember that a chair must have all four legs to be fully functional. Our final support in our spiritual journey is *discipline*. *Discipline* is: training that *corrects*, *molds*, or *perfects* the mental faculties or moral character. It is an orderly conduct or pattern of behavior. *Discipline* may often be related to having *structure* in one's life.

Exercise:

Think about and make a list of what you feel are your top seven *greatest achievements* you have accomplished during your lifetime.

1._____

2._____

3._____

4._____

5._____

6._____

7._____

Now look at each of these achievements and rank on a scale of 1-10 how much discipline was required for you to accomplish each one. Then write for each one the top *three* key activities that you did to attain each achievement.

1._____

_____

_____

2._____

_____

_____

3._____

_____

_____

4._____

_____

_____

5._____

_____

_____

6._____

_____

_____

7._____

_____

_____

Now look at each activity above. How many of the accomplishments did you score at a level of a 7 or above?_____

Now look at all of the three key activities that you listed for each of the seven achievements. Circle any that are the same. List any key activities that you notice are the same below. Then list any key activities that you notice are similar._____

_____

_____

_____

_____

_____

_____

_____

_____

_____

What are any other common features you notice above? Describe how you feel your level of *discipline* has played a role in your life to accomplish your highest achievements?_____

_____

_____

_____

_____

_____

Reading Assignment: Read pages 207-215 including *You Are Your Possibilites.*

Exercise:

Take the next seven days to journal your daily routine and activities throughout each day. Write down the time you do each activity throughout your day. Detail each different type of activity. Example: 6:00am woke up, 6:15 Sat in meditation, 7:00 Ate breakfast and got ready for work, 8:30 At my office working, 11:30 At a staff meeting, 12:30 Ate lunch, 1:00 Sat in meditation,

1:30 Working again, 5:30 went to gym and lifted weights and 20 mins walking on treadmill, 6:30 went home and cooked/ate dinner, 8:00 wash a load of laundry/watch a tv show with my spouse/partner, 9:00 finish folding laundry and read my new spiritual book, 10:15 went to bed. Obviously, this is what might look like a day during a workday. However, a weekend day will most likely look different. Write down each different type of activity and the time you began to do each similar to above for each day below. If there is not enough room below, use another piece of paper. This may seem like it is a little tedious. But it will really help us to get a really great snapshot of our life that we may not be able to visualize in any other way.

Time:	Day 1:	Day 2:	Day 3:	Day 4:	Day 5:	Day 6:	Day 7:

After finishing your seven days of journaling, take a few minutes to step back and take a closer look. Try to imagine that you are viewing this week's snapshot of your life through the eyes of an outside observer. Imagine that this person is someone who holds the highest and greatest deal of love and support for you. S(he) is someone who wishes to see you accomplish your greatest purpose and potential in life and be fully happy. Now that you are that other person, first look to see if there is an identifiable *structure*. Do you go to bed and get up at about the same time each day and night? Are you getting at least 7-8 hours sleep each night? Are you eating your meals at about the same time daily? Are you eating three *healthy* meals each day? Do you have some form of activity that exercises your body? If so, is there some regular routine during the week? Do you have a regular work/service time? Do you always arrive on time and perform all of your responsibilities fully? Do I have a regular spiritual practice? Do I practice at the same times each day? Am I involved in a Spiritual Community? Do I have a regular routine to participate in my community? Do I have a regular routine to do activities with my family? What activities am I doing for my own growth? Do I do these regularly? What are my hobbies or other activities I do for fun? Are these in my schedule? Answer these questions below after looking at reviewing your week as a caring outsider.

_____

_____

_____

_____

_____

_____

_____

_____

_____

_____

Look at each of the activities from your seven day journal above, and describe anything else that you may have noticed with the overall structure of your week._____

_____

_____

_____

Now look at each of the activities from your journal above, and write down each type of activity into the category in which it belongs. Example: Eating breakfast, Eating lunch would each be written down into the health category. Going to a movie with your kids would be written under the family category. Practicing meditation would be listed under spiritual growth. Going on a hike with your partner might go under hobby, relationship, and health. *If you do the activity multiple times during the week, only write it down once into it's proper category.*

Family:

1._____

2._____

3._____

4._____

5._____

6._____

7._____

8._____

9._____

Health:

1._____

2._____

3._____

4._____

5._____

6._____

7._____

8._____

9._____

Hobbies:

1._____

2._____

3._____

4._____

5._____

6._____

7._____

8._____

9._____

Relationship:

1._____

2._____

3._____

4._____

5._____

6._____

7._____

8._____

9._____

Spiritual Growth:

1._____

2._____

3._____

4._____

5._____

6._____

7._____

8._____

9._____

Career/Education:

1._____

2._____

3._____

4._____

5._____

6._____

7._____

8._____

9._____

Look at each of the categories above. Does it look balanced? Is there one or more categories in which you seem to have a larger number of activities? Is there one or more categories in which you have few or no activities listed? Which ones?_____

_____

_____

Now look back at the common key activities that you circled in the previous exercise which were key to your attaining your greatest accomplishments in life. Are any of those activities the same, or similar to the ones you recorded above in your week's journal? If so, which one's? If not, why do you think they are missing?_____

_____

_____

_____

_____

_____

Now start at the top of your list, and for each activity look back at your original seven day journal to notice, and remind yourself how well structured/not well structured the activity is during your week. Keeping this in mind, think about the activity and ask yourself how much dedication you feel towards it and how well/not so well this is reflected in your seven day journal. Then on a scale of 1-10, rate how you feel your level of dedication/commitment is to this activity. (1 is the lowest level of dedication/commitment to the activity and 10 is the greatest level of dedication/commitment towards the activity) Example: Eating breakfast: (I notice from my journal that I am eating breakfast everyday usually at 7:00, and it is a healthy meal. My feelings are that I have a high level of importance and dedication to eating breakfast as a daily routine and healthy food.) I would score this a 10. Going for a hike with my partner: (I notice from my journal that I did this activity once, and placed it under relationship, hobby, and health. Since this was one of only two quality activities during the week with my partner, I would score my level of dedication to this activity in my relationship at a 6. Under the health category, I notice that besides this activity, I have had at least 4 other activities during the week which involved physical activity. I would score my level of dedication to this activity in my health at an 8. Under the hobbies category, I notice that this is the only activity during the week I entered as a hobby. Therefore, I would score my level of dedication to this activity in my hobbies as a 4.) Write your 1-10 score at the end of each individual activity you listed above. Now add up each score for each category below and obtain the total. Then divide into this number the total number of activities you scored. Write this total for each of the categories. Example: If you have five activities listed for *family*, and you scored each activity a 7, 9, 6, 8 and a 5. Add them together: 7+9+6+8+5=35. Next divide the number of activities into the total. 35÷5=7.0. If you have any categories in which you did not list *any* activities, you will score a 0 for that category.

Family: _____ + _____ + _____ + _____ + _____ + _____ + _____ + _____ + _____ = _____

(Total) _____ ÷ (Number Activities)_____ = _____

Health: _____ + _____ + _____ + _____ + _____ + _____ + _____ + _____ + _____ = _____

(Total) _____ ÷ (Number Activities)_____ = _____

Hobbies: _____ + _____ + _____ + _____ + _____ + _____ + _____ + _____ + _____ = _____

(Total) _____ ÷ (Number Activities)_____ = _____

Relationship: _____ + _____ + _____ + _____ + _____ + _____ + _____ + _____ + _____ = _____

(Total) _____ ÷ (Number Activities)_____ = _____

Spiritual Growth: : _____ + _____ + _____ + _____ + _____ + _____ + _____ + _____ + _____ = _____

(Total) _____ ÷ (Number Activities)_____ = _____

Career/Education: : _____ + _____ + _____ + _____ + _____ + _____ + _____ + _____ + _____ = _____

(Total) _____ ÷ (Number Activities)_____ = _____

Now write your *average* for each key area below:

Family:_____

Health: _____

Hobbies: _____

Relationship: _____

Spiritual Growth:_____

Career/Education:_____

Look at your average scores in each key area above. Your scores will be from a 0-10. Each score represents to you what your *present level* of discipline is in each of these key areas. If you have a score of a 0 in one of the areas, this indicates that you currently *have no* dedication in your life to this area. If you have a 1-4 you currently have *minimal* dedication/discipline in this area of your life. If you have a 5-6 you presently have *some* dedication/discipline in this area of your life. If you scored at a 7-8 you presently have a *moderately high* level of dedication/discipline in this area of your life. If you scored at a 9-10 you presently have the *highest level* of dedication/discipline in this area of your life.

Circle any of the areas above in which you scored less than a 7. Look at each key area and discuss what of this has surprised you in any way. Describe anything else that you have noticed._____

_____

_____

_____

Now look at the areas you circled. Are there any that you feel you would like/need to improve? Choose *two* areas you would like to improve in your *discipline*. Then list *two* activities you feel you could begin to add, or change during your daily/weekly routine in life for each of the two areas. List them below. Example: *Health*: I am going to bed every night before 10:30. I am taking a healthy lunch from home to work each day. *Spiritual Growth*: I am practicing meditation each morning for 30 minutes at 6:30. I am reading uplifting spiritual books that I enjoy for 30 minutes before bedtime each night. Use an *I am* statement for each one and be as specific as possible in detail for each activity.

1st Key Area: _____

I am_____

_____

I am_____

_____

2nd Key Area:_____

I am_____

_____

I am_____

_____

Now choose *one* activity from the 1st key area, and *one* from the 2nd key area. Write both of the affirmations down on two note cards and place it on your bathroom mirror and refrigerator. Be sure to notice these and read them each time you go into the bathroom and refrigerator. Describe below how you plan to incorporate these into your daily/weekly routine. Then take action and begin. Once you have successfully added these two to your routine(you have been doing the activities for at least 5-6 weeks), you may do the same as above with the other two activities.___

_____

_____

_____

_____

_____

Since beginning these exercises, have you had any other realizations or thoughts on *discipline* in your life? If so, describe these. _____

_____

_____

_____

_____

Homework:

At the bottom of your paper of affirmations write *I am living life with Discipline.* Neatly affix your affirmation paper on your bathroom mirror and refrigerator. Continue to *imagine, state* and *think* each of your affirmations each time you go into the refrigerator and also while you are brushing your teeth each day.

Continue to pay attention to any new insights that you notice during these two weeks and write them in your notebook.

Buddy Call:

Take turns sharing with your partner a couple of your great achievements you listed above. Share what you noticed about the key elements which were common in some of your accomplishments. Share if you noticed those same key elements in your week of activity journaling. Share two of your strongest areas in which you discovered you have the greatest areas of *discipline.* Then share two of your weakest areas in which you discovered a lesser degree of *discipline.* Share the two affirmations you created to practice more discipline and your plan of action to move this into your life. Describe and share any other realizations or breakthroughs you had as a result of doing this work on *discipline.*

11

Powertools For The Path

Reading Assignment: Read pages 216 – 219 including *The Seven Sacred Flames.*

Key Concept:

You now have a fundamental understanding that *everything* in our surrounding world is *Energy,* and that our *thoughts, words, feelings,* and *actions* also are creative *Energies.* Now you have practiced meditation, and have experienced first-hand much of the fundamental benefits available to you through this regular practice. So it is time to dip into the more esoteric teachings and practices of the Great Masters of history. Truly every person who came here and became a *Master,* was taught and eventually *mastered* through regular practice these teachings of the *Seven Sacred Flames.* Many years ago, this information was shrouded and only given to a select few who were deemed ready. Today this information is now available to everyone, and anyone who practices using these energies regularly can also attain *mastery* in one's life.

Each of these flames are energies which are available to everyone and are eternal. They are not visible to us through the five ordinary senses, nevertheless are present for our use. Also with a little practice during meditation, it is possible to experience each flame's very pronounced synergy. And yes, it is possible to *see* eventually these flames. Rather than attempting to initially learn several of the flames, during this course we will focus on *one* of the primary flames.

Exercise:

In the book I described Yogis in India who have been seen to master the unseen energy of gravity by levitating in the air during meditation. All of our high technologies of today use unseen energies to create audible and visible sounds and images. We don't need to look past the tv, computer, smart phones or any electic device to see there is an *unseen network* we can tap into. Likewise, there are other unseen energies in which our *thoughts, words, feelings* and *actions* influence. Describe below at least two incidents in which you *thought, felt, or spoke* words which influenced an unexpected action or event to occur in your life. This may be anything large or small that you noticed or seemed unusual._____

_____

_____

_____

_____

_____

_____

Now look at the two events you wrote about above. Do you feel it is probable in each event or action that the *energy* of your thoughts, feelings, or words *influenced* or in any other way acted upon any sort of other *unseen energy?* Can you see this is possible? If yes, explain why._____

_____

_____

_____

_____

Reading Assignment: Read pages 219-229 including *The Violet Transmuting Flame. Benefits and Actions of The Flame,* and *Clouds and Angels.*

Key Concept:

There are *Seven Sacred Flames.* The seventh flame or ray is called *The Violet Flame of Transmutation.* The Ascended Master Saint Germain is in charge of this ray. Each of the different rays have unique qualities and actions. Some of the main qualities and actions of the Violet flame include: freedom, transmutation, transformation, diplomacy, and application of the science of alchemy. The color which is associated with this ray is violet. The main role of the

Violet Flame is that of *transmutation*. *Transmutation* is the action of changing and/or converting a lower energy and/or substance into a higher energy and/or substance. This energy can be activated and placed into any situation in your life. It can be put into your health, relationships, career, finances, family, karma, and any other situation you wish to transform and improve.

Exercise:

Make a list below of seven situations in your life you would most like to experience transformation in your life. Rank them in order of 1-7 in highest prior to the lowest priority. Try to be as specific as possible. Poor Example: I would like to transform my relationships.(This example is too general) Good Example: I would like to transform my relationship with my partner/spouse and improve our communication.(This example is more specific.)

1._____

2._____

3._____

4._____

5._____

6._____

7._____

Reading Assignment: Read pages 229-223 including *Making the Call,* and *Decrees and Invocations.*

Key Concept:

It is important to remember that utilizing this tool is the same as utilizing any spiritual tool we have available to us. These are our invisible lifelines. However, first we must understand and *know* they are there for our use. Secondly, we must understand *how* to use them. Then we must *remember* to use them. It is important to know that the *Violet Flame* is available always, but we must first *make the call.* Then it is similar to any tool; we must practice. *Regular practice* creates results.

Exercise:

Write below the following decree: *I am the Violet Transmuting Flame in Manifestation and Action!* Write it below.

_____

At the beginning of your meditation for the next 4 days invoke the violet flame. As always, use the full feeling of you thoughts and words. State this on the first day three times. On the second day of meditation invoke this decree nine times. On the 3rd and 4th days invoke this decree 16 times. Write below anything you experienced during your meditations during these four days below._____

_____

_____

_____

_____

_____

_____

_____

_____

Exercise:

Look at your seven situations you listed above in the previous exercise you would like to experience transformation. Select #1 and go to page 230-231 in the book under *Decrees and Invocations*. Use these as a template, and choose whichever of the six examples best fits for your #1. Write below your new decree. Example: You wish to improve your relationship with your boss, Sandy Smith. You write: *I invoke the Violet Transmuting Flame into every aspect of my relationship with Sandy Smith. I invoke the Violet Flame to transmute everything within this relationship that does not serve into pure light and love, and that which does serve. I invoke that this flame shall be continuously activated and energized, continuously established, and continuously anchored throughout every aspect of this relationship. By the grace of my beloved Saint Germain, and so it is!*

_____

_____

_____

_____

_____

_____

_____

_____

_____

Now take this new invocation into your meditation each day. Same as above, put a high level of feeling into the invocation as you think and speak the decree. State them three times in the beginning of your medition. Also imagine *seeing* the energy of the violet flame penetrating this situation. This should take about the first 4-5 minutes of your meditation. Then you may continue during the rest of your meditation with whatever you choose. Continue to do this every day in your meditation for the next 7-10 days. Write down anything you notice during your meditation. Write any shift you may notice in the situation and write these below and in your journal._____

_____

_____

_____

_____

_____

_____

_____

Often there are *sudden situations* which may occur in our life which are appropriate to invoke the *Violet Flame.* During the next few days, notice if there are any such situations in your life. Examples might be: An argument occurs between two people at work. A driver gets angry at you and cusses you in traffic. You walk across the room and stub your toe on your dresser, and your toe is swelling. You may create an instant decree to invoke the violet flame. You don't have to say it out loud if the situation doesn't allow it. It is just as powerful to simply use your thoughts. Your invocation can be simple: I invoke the violet flame to move into this argument with ___ and __. I invoke the violet flame to surround me and this driver with love and light and to transmute anything not serving. I invoke the violet flame to move into every aspect of my toe and transmute anything not serving. Remember that these don't have to be perfect, and it is always ready for us to call. Find a situation or two in the next few days and practice instantly calling the violet flame for assistance. Write about the situations, what you did, and what you noticed afterwards._____

_____

_____

_____

_____

_____

_____

_____

Look at your seven situations you listed above in the previous exercise you would like to experience transformation. Select #2 and go to page 230-231 in the book under *Decrees and Invocations*. Use these as a template, and choose whichever of the six examples best fits for your #2. You may wish to copy this section so you may continue each week with #3 through #7 of your list. Write below your new decree._____

_____

_____

_____

_____

_____

_____

_____

Now take this new invocation into your meditation each day. Same as above, put much feeling into the invocation as you think and speak the decree. State them three times in the beginning of your medition. Also imagine *seeing* the energy of the violet flame penetrating this situation. This should take about the first 4-5 minutes of your meditation. Then you may continue during the rest of your medition with whatever you choose. Continue to do this every day in your meditation for the next 7-10 days. Write down anything you notice during your meditation. Write any shifting you may notice in the situation and write these below and in your journal._____

_____

_____

_____

_____

_____

_____

_____

_____

Homework:

Continue every 7-10 days creating a new Violet Flame decree for use during the first 4-5 minutes of your meditation each day until you move through your whole list of seven. Pay attention and journal any *aha moments* or realizations. Look at what you are noticing specifically in the situations you are working with the violet flame. Be sure to *simply allow* the situation to shift in its own way and time. Often the shifts may come in unexpected ways. Pay attention and journal your experiences. As with any tool, it simply takes some practice. When we are consistent, so is this energy. Also, look for other ways to use this tool in your everyday life as sudden situations pop up.

Buddy Call:

Take turns sharing with your buddy this week what you noticed when you first practiced using the *Violet Flame* during your meditation the first 3-4 days. Then share what situation you chose to use the *Violet Flame.* Share the experiences that you had both during your meditation and any shifts you noticed in the situation as a result. Also, share the couple of times you practiced using the *Violet Flame* in your day to day life situations, and what you experienced.

12

The Spiral Ladder We Climb

Reading Assignment: Read pages 234-236.

Key Concept: Deoxyribonucleic Acid, or DNA is a component of every cell in every living organism. It carries information and is shaped as a *double helix.* Not only do we find this spiral shape inside of the cells throughout all of nature, we also visibly can see this same pattern outside of the cells in nature as well. Once we are trained, we can learn to see that this spiral pattern occurs in every area of our life.

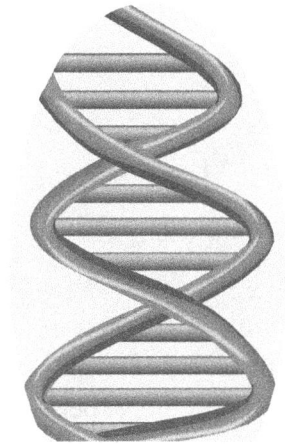

Exercise

Take about 10 minutes to go outside and look for as many living organisms as possible that you can see the spiral pattern. Write them down below. Keep looking until you find at least 5 different things.

1._____

2._____

3._____

4._____

5._____

Now go outside and look at any birds you may see. Try to find them in an open space such as a field. Watch them as they are flying. Wait until you can watch at least 3-4 different birds flying. Really pay attention to how they fly *closely*. What do you see? Can you notice any pattern in any of them? What pattern do you notice?_____

_____

_____

_____

Reading Assignment: Read pages 237-249 including *The Perfect Spiral, The Relationship Diagram,* and *Analyzing Our Spirals.*

Key Concept: Now that we can see throughout our bodies and all of nature there are spiral patterns, it makes sense for us to recognize that this same pattern exists in our *relationships* with everything. The challenge here is to first of all know that these exist, secondly to be able to *identify* these in our life, and then to truly understand what is the life lesson beneath the surface. Lastly, once we understand the lesson, how do we move through it in an easier, and softer way. To figure this out we have to take a really good look at our past and present, and be an impartial judge of ourselves. Once again, we must step away and look at our life from the eyes of an outsider.

Exercise:

We know that often the lessons we currently are working on may show up in our life in some form of *conflict*. They may show up in a large way, or smaller way. They show up for the same reason and repeat over and over. The only difference is that each time they may show up in a different part of your life, and simply dressed differently with a different person. Choose the top three people/relationships/areas in which you are experiencing the greatest amount of conflict in your life right now. Be very specific in the seeming reason and write them below in the order of greatest to least amount of conflict. Example: There is conflict right now with my co-worker,_____ at my office. We are on the same marketing team and disagree all of the time with marketing strategies, and argue about many different things. We argue over what our boss said she wants us to do for an assignment. When staff was asked what color to paint the breakroom, we took opposite sides even on colors. We seem to oppose each other all of the time.

1._____

_____

_____

_____

_____

_____

2._____

_____

_____

_____

_____

_____

_____

3._____

_____

_____

_____

_____

_____

Now look at the #1 conflict you listed and described above. How long has this conflict been occuring? 2 weeks, 2 months, 2 years, etc. Write the amount of time this has been occuring.

Now, think back to before this conflict began and look at the *two year* time period just before this conflict first began. Can you think of any other conflicts you had during this time-frame that seemed similar to this one? If so, write down the details of this conflict below same as you did above. If you did not notice a similar conflict within a two year time frame, then move the time-frame out to three years. If you do not notice a similar conflict, move it out to four years and so on until you do find a similar conflict and write its details below._____

_____

_____

_____

_____

_____

_____

Now do the same thing as above. Look at the time period of between 2-3 years *before* the conflict you detailed just above. Was there *another* conflict that seemed similar to this one? If not within 2-3 years, look back even further until you find another conflict. Write out its details below._____

_____

_____

_____

_____

_____

_____

Now look at the *three different*, yet similar conflicts you have detailed above. See if you can notice any similarities. What are they? Write them below. What are the similar actions the other person(s) seemed to take during the conflict? List them. What are the similar actions/thoughts/words/feelings you have during the conflict? List those._____

_____

_____

_____

_____

_____

_____

During the next three days, take these three different, yet similar activities in your life into your meditation. Review each of these for 2-3 minutes before beginning your meditation each day. Then simply be open to receiving any guidance, realizations, and assistance to help you to *discern* how these activities are connected. Pay attention during, immediately after, and for the next few days to any possible direct and indirect messages from other people and situations. Set your intention that you will see the underlying connection between these conflicts, and will be able to recognize the true lesson. Write everything you notice below._____

_____

_____

_____

_____

_____

_____

After you have spent *at least* three days contemplating these, see if you can answer these questions. What is the *quality* of energy I have placed into these situations? What is the *quality* of energy I am receiving back in these situations? Are the energies based in *fear* or *love*? What is the lesson I have the opportunity to learn?_____

_____

_____

_____

_____

_____

Write your own decree for this current situation in your life with the Violet Flame below. Now go into meditation again. Invoke the Violet Flame into this current situation. Then ask, *What can I do to lessen this conflict in my life and to create a shift in myself?* Pay attention during and after your meditations for the next couple of days and write all that you notice below._____

_____

_____

_____

_____

_____

_____

_____

_____

Write below *two* action steps you plan to take to create a shift in this situation. Remember, that this is truly an exercise of learning *discernment*. There is no easy way for us to analyze the conflicts in our life without attempting to move out of our own skin for a moment, and see as an outsider. Also by going within, this allows us to shed the ego and see the highest part of our true nature for the answers. The *regular practice* of *discernment* leads us towards a greater attainment of *wisdom*. It is only through *consistent practice* which will allow us to move more easily through our life. Make sure you create an *I am* statement. Then put them both into action immediately. Example: Let's say that I was able to connect that I had three conflicts with quite a few similarities. Each seemed to be with a co-worker or boss. I determined after one of my meditations that I seemed to be in a pattern of feeling that the other person didn't respect my opinion and take it into consideration. I was able to see that I also treated him the same by cutting him off in conversations, which lead to arguments over most things. So I was able to *discern* that in order for others to respect my opinions, I needed to respect the opinions of others as well. My two action steps: I am every day telling my co-worker_____, one thing that I appreciate about him. I am at each meeting allowing my co-worker_____ to completely speak on his ideas, and listening fully without cutting him off.

1._____

_____

2._____

_____

Take a look at this conflict *1-2 weeks* after you have placed these two action steps into practice. Has the conflict shifted? How so? Describe below._____

_____

_____

_____

_____

Next look at your #2 conflict above and go through the same process with the next conflict. Now that you have practiced this with your highest charged conflict, the others will become easier. As mentioned before, with more practice it will become easier to spot and connect the patterns. Soon it will become almost like second nature. When you notice a new conflict that seems to bubble up, you will more easily recognize it is one of your spiral patterns, and start working to resolve it. Then the resolutions will become easier each time. Another thing to realize, is once we learn and move through one type of lesson, there are more to come on its heels. This lets us know that we are truly evolving and moving forward. As mentioned before, we are truly on a never ending *journey* in which there is no end.

Now look at the #2 conflict you listed and described above. How long has this conflict been occuring? 2 weeks, 2 months, 2 years, etc. Write the amount of time this has been occuring. Now, think back to before this conflict began and look at the *two year* time period just before this conflict first began. Can you think of any other conflicts you had during this time-frame that seemed similar to this one? If so, write down the details of this conflict below same as you did above. If you did not notice a similar conflict within a two year time frame, then move the time out to three years. If you do not notice a similar conflict, move it out to four years and so on until you do find a similar conflict and write its details below._____

_____

_____

_____

_____

_____

_____

_____

Now do the same thing as above. Look at the time period of between 2-3 years before the conflict you detailed just above. Was there *another* conflict that seemed similar to this one? If not within 2-3 years, look back even further until you find another conflict. Write out its details below._____

_____

_____

_____

_____

_____

_____

Now look at the three different, yet similar conflicts you have detailed above. See if you can notice any similarities. What are they? Write them below. What are the similar actions the other person(s) seemed to take during the conflict? List them. What are the similar actions/thoughts/words/feelings you have during the conflict? List those._____

_____

_____

_____

_____

During the next three days, take these three different similar activities in your life into your meditation. Review each of these for 2-3 minutes before beginning your meditation each day. Then simply be open to receiving any guidance, realizations, and assistance to help you to *discern* how these activities are connected. Pay attention during, immediately after, and for the next few days to any possible direct and indirect messages from other people and situations. Set your intention that you will see the underlying connection between these conflicts, and will be able to recognize the true lesson. Write everything you notice below._____

_____

_____

_____

_____

_____

_____

_____

After you have spent *at least* three days contemplating these, see if you can answer these questions. What is the *quality* of energy I have placed into these situations? What is the *quality* of energy I am receiving back in these situations? What is the lesson I have the opportunity to learn?_____

_____

_____

_____

_____

_____

Write your own decree for your current situation in your life with the Violet Flame below. Now go into meditation again. Invoke the Violet Flame into this current situation. Then ask, *What can I do to lessen this conflict in my life and to create a shift in myself?* Pay attention during and after for the next couple of days and write all that you notice below._____

_____

_____

_____

_____

_____

_____

_____

Write below *two* action steps you plan to take to create a shift in this situation. Remember, that this is truly an exercise of learning *discernment.* There is no easy way for us to analyze the conflicts in our life without attempting to move out of our own skin for a moment, and see as an outsider. Also by going within, this allows us to shed the ego and see the highest part of our true nature for the answers. The *regular practice* of *discernment* leads us towards a greater attainment of *wisdom.* It is only through consistent practice which will allow us to move more easily through our life. Make sure you create an *I am* statement. Then put them both into action immediately. Example: I was able to connect that I had three conflicts with quite a few similarities. Each occurred in my current and two previous romantic relationships. I determined after one of my meditations that I seemed to be in a pattern in each of these relationships. I was able to see that our arguments always involved my spending more time working later in the evenings. I didn't understand why it was such a big deal to my partner. I noticed that we would have major conflicts because I wasn't available to take any vacations throughout the year. I always felt that this wasn't such a big deal. But it was a big deal to my partner, and there was constant conflict. So after taking some time to *listen,* I was able to *discern* after distancing myself, that it was really important for my partner to take occasional vacations with me. Also, I was able to see that instead of spending quality time with my partner I was choosing to work. Therefore, I realized I was short-changing my relationship with my partner. And I was shorting my own health by not allowing a proper amount of time for rest. My two action steps: I am planning at least one major vacation, and two smaller vacations with my partner_____ during the next year. I am diligent in leaving my work each day before or at 6:30 so I may spend more time relaxing with my partner_____ and family.

1._____

_____

2._____

Take a look at this conflict 1-2 weeks after you have placed these two action steps into practice. Has the confict shifted? How so? Describe below._____

_____

_____

_____

_____

Homework

Continue doing the work above with your 2nd conflict, and then eventually your 3rd conflict as well. Pay attention to the things that come up and you notice. It is important to *allow* these relationships to shift in their own time. There is no need to push to make anything happen. Simply be open and aware. Write anything in your journal that you notice. There may be other insights that come to you even later during this process. Pay attention to everything that you notice. Also remember that you can repeat this process with any new conflict that you notice.

Practice putting the Violet Flame into these situations as well. Write down any new realizations that you have noticed with any of this work, or that of the previous weeks.

Buddy Call

Take turns sharing with your buddy what things you found outside in nature that displayed spirals. Then share what you were able to see when you watched different birds flying. Next, share your #1 conflict that you took with you into meditation. Share what you noticed. Share what pattern you found occuring over and over in previous situations. What part of the conflict did you discover you were contributing? Discuss whether you were able to see that the other person(s) were mirroring back your feelings and energy of the situation. Share your two action step statements with your partner and the action you have taken. What have you noticed since taking the steps? Discuss any changes you have noticed. Share with your partner any large *aha moments* or realizations you have had during the last two weeks.

This ends the formal portion of sharing and completing this workbook. However, you and your buddy may wish to remain in contact and continue to check in with each other as you continue on your journey. There are suggestions on how to continue the *transformational* work in the afterword, and how to approach what's next. There are certain portions of this workbook which are designed to be repeated. Since our lives are continuously unfolding with new opportunities for growth and evolution, it is entirely appropriate to go back and go through the exercises again. It is important to remember that every Great Master has one major thing in common; it took a lot of *practicing.* That is ultimately the way for us each to have our own *Transformational* experiences and to *Awaken!*

Afterword

As I sit here about to finish this *Transformational Workbook,* I am so greatly reminded of just how easy it is to become sidetracked during this Age of high-tech everything. I thought I would finish this workbook in a few short months after completing my book *Love Yourself and Be Healed:Awakening.* It is now *over two years* since I published my first book. You might be asking, "So what happened?" When I use a little bit of *discernment* in my life and walk over to those bleachers at a distance and look in, it becomes so clear.

I went to see my beloved Sai Maa in Florida just over a month ago. She had invited all 3500 of the graduates of a very intensive program she had spent about ten years teaching. It was the end of this Era of her teaching this specific program. There were at least 700 of us there and we were being given a reminder of the key elements of the program and how to continue to practice doing the work. During one portion of the program we were to choose a person from our present or past we felt we needed to practice going through the steps and doing more work. I sat for a moment and really couldn't think of everyone. I thought to myself, *I know I have gone through all of my major relationships and the ones I can think of from the past....*Then someone popped suddenly into my head from my past. I thought, *well, we are just practicing. I am sure I cleared that person. I'll just use them for practice.* The person who popped into my head was an authority figure who had said some fairly critical things to me at the ripe age of 21. As a child at age 7 and up, I wrote stories for fun. I would write *and complete* all types of stories. I would do the writing assignments which were required for my English classes and write more. During college I finally discovered my major in Communications and wrote for the college newspaper. I discovered I loved to write feature articles. While in college I wrote a feature length article which was not any sort of assignment, but it was simply for fun. I submitted it to our local newspaper. I was so excited because they published it. It was one full page of the newspaper. I graduated from college and submitted my resume to that same local newspaper. I was excited to have an interview with the Editor. During the interview he told me, "You really don't have enough talent to write for the newspaper. I would suggest that you take some more writing classes as you need to practice quite a bit more." I asked why he had published my story if my writing was so bad. He stated,"We did that as a favor to your college instructor who used to work here. We had to *really* edit your story to be able to use it. It really wasn't good enough initially to meet our standards." I thanked him for his time, and had no idea that one encounter such as that could get me sidetracked from *ever finishing* another piece of writing for at least 30 years. My college teacher told me I should ignore what he said. I looked over my original article finding they only edited two words in the entire full page spread. That same last year of college I had won several Kentucky Intercollegiate Press Association Awards for my writing. Yet I still apparently absorbed his words and they had influenced me enough to *never finish* another significant piece of writing. I had previously *done the work* surrounding this incident with this person from my past about four years earlier. I was able to clear the 30 year *writer's block* which had moved between myself and my passion. Yeahhh!!! So I even wrote about this after finally

122

writing my first book. Everything seemed great. But then something happened....I started writing the companion workbook I had promised my readers I would finish in 3-4 months. I got to chapter 8 of the workbook and stopped. It was easy to explain, this or that or the other kept me busy and I was sidetracked for two years! Was that the real reason? It's the one I told myself.

So I sat in the retreat and went through the steps to *do the work* with this man from my past. No big deal, as I thought I had cleared this all before. Next thing I knew, there were tears and emotions bubbling up almost stronger than I remember from the first time. I *couldn't believe* I *still had stuff* there with him to clear! I just did the work and allowed all of the emotions to come anyway and shared with my partner. As I sat wading through my feelings, I realized I had allowed this *one person* whom I had a 20 minute encounter to take away one of my *primary passions* and *purposes* in my life!

This was a great reminder that sometimes the events/conflicts we have had from the past with other people may need to be revisited. We may think that we have finished and cleared something, yet it is possible to still have some branches that can regrow to entangle us in our life. How do we know that we need to go back and do more work with something? If I had been instructed to *make it a regular practice* to systematically go back through and look at the *present* and *past* of my life on a continuous basis, it is likely that this would have come to the surface quicker for me to clear.

I *did the work* again for this event from my past about 5 weeks ago. I sit here even while going through the busy holiday season having completed the final 4 chapters of this workbook. I already am anxiously looking forward to planning and writing my next book.

We really never have any idea when an event from long ago in our past, or one which recently occurred is having some sort of effect on us. It could be either stopping us or slowing us down in any number of ways from fully expressing who we came here to be. We each have our own *Divine Purpose.* We bring our own unique gifts and talents to express here.

Truly the intention of my first book and this workbook is to provide each person with a systematic step-by-step approach to bring *Transformation* into their lives and to *Awaken.* What exactly does that look like? It will be completely different for each person. However, for *every* person it is for us to live our lives more *fully*. What are the blocks standing in our way that need to be moved? What is it that brings us the most *passion*? What is it that brings us the most *love*? What is ours to *give*? What is ours to *receive*? After completing this book and workbook, you will have found these answers and more. These tools, solutions, and so much more are all here waiting for us. Remember that we each are here on a *journey* and there is *never* any finish line.

Tips For Perpetual Study and Continuous Growth

After you have completed this workbook, I highly recommend that you periodically go back through most of the exercises and do them again. Our lives are dynamic and constantly changing. Occasionally, there are branches that come back again from our past for us to clear once more. Also, we have a continuous stream of events occuring in our day to day lives. It is important to take 15-20 minutes at least 2-4 days each week to devote to *doing the work again*. Be sure to keep your journal and write down every new idea, inspiration, and *aha moment* you notice.

Also, if you and your *buddy* decided to remain in contact, you can decide whether you wish to schedule a *buddy call* every two, or three weeks to continue sharing your progress. If you did not stay in contact, feel free to find another friend that you might share in the same way on a call.

Below is the suggested schedule and assignments. I suggest that you complete each of the assignments during a two week time period. In this manner you will repeat all of the essentials from the course roughly every eight months.

Assignment 1:

Review chapter 3 and complete the first two exercises on events which have occurred during the last month. Do the three exercises on the current teachers in your life in chapter 3. Read and do the homework listed for chapter 3.

Assignment 2:

Review chapter 4 and complete the last 6 exercises on fear and love. Read and do the homework listed for chapter 4.

Assignment 3:

Review chapter 5 and complete the first 11 exercises.

Assignment 4:

Review chapter 5 and complete the day #1- day #7 exercises and the next exercise immediately following.

Assignment 5:

Review chapter 5 and complete the seven exercises on *selflessness*. Read and do the homework listed for chapter 5.

Assignment 6:

Review chapter 6 and complete the five exercises on *compassion*. Complete the eight exercises on *giving*.

Assignment 7:

Review chapter 6 and complete the exercises on *talents, treasures* and *tithing* and complete the homework listed for chapter 6.

Assignment 8:

Review chapter 7 and complete the five exercises on *receiving.*

Assignment 9:

Review chapter 7 and practice again the section on *breathing meditation* and *mantra meditation.* Practice and write a new mantra for use in your meditation. Complete the next six exercises related to your *tree of complaints* and *tree of gratitudes.*

Assignment 10:

Review chapter 8 and read all of your answers you wrote for the exercises in this section on *passion* and *power.* Look at the list of activities you listed in which you have *passion.* How many of these were you able to implement back into your life? Take at least two action steps to bring one of these activities into your life. Complete the homework at the end of this chapter.

Assignment 11:

Review chapter 9 and complete the first six exercise sections. Then choose *two* of the events you listed and complete an *event worksheet* on each one.

Assignment 12:

Review chapter 9 and select at least *five* more of the events you listed and complete an *event worksheet* on each one. Then complete the last two exercises in the chapter. Complete the homework at the end of the chapter.

Assignment 13:

Review chapter 10 and read through all of your exercises that you finished previously on *discipline.* Look at the exercise where you listed the *two key areas* in which you would like to improve your discipline. How well have you been doing lately? Take *two action steps* that will help you to increase your level of discipline in one of the key areas you listed. Complete the homework at the end of the chapter.

Assignment 14:

Review chapter 11 and complete the exercise section on your top 7 areas of your life you would like to transform. Then complete the next seven exercises and practice using the Violet Flame on these situations. Complete the homework at the end of the chapter.

Assignment 15:

Review chapter 12 and complete the exercise listing the top three conflicts in your life right now. Then complete the next seven exercises for conflict #1.

Assignment 16:

Review chapter 12 and complete for conflict #2 the next seven exercises for conflict #2.

Assignment 17:

Review chapter 12 and complete for conflict #3 the next seven exercises for conflict #3. Complete the homework at the end of the chapter.

Dedication

I am so grateful for the realization that we are on a never-ending journey. Without this knowledge I am sure it would be much easier to simply give up and allow myself to get distracted in any of the countless ways possible. I would not have come to this realization without the divine grace of my beloved H.H. Sai Maa. I owe her much more than I am sure I can even recognize. I have truly *received* so many teachings and awakenings through her Divine support and love.

I thank my parents who have been my steadfast support through my life. It is their love that was my first display and experience of unconditional love. I am forever grateful you said *yes* to bring me here and give me the perfect experience I needed. You both are my greatest teachers of all by showing me how to live life and by being my loving parents.

I am so thankful for my brother giving me encouragement. You were 12 and I was eight when you read one of my stories and told me,"It was good and you should keep writing!" I am so grateful you encouraged me back then and throughout the years in everything I ever have aspired to do in my life.

And I am so grateful that my childhood friend is now my partner/spouse. You are the one who was willing to explore one church and religion after another with me as a teenager. We waded our way through at least 20 different churches and religions during that year. After many circumstances separated us for over 25 years, we finally reconnected to discover that we both continued our *meaning of life* search separately. We amazingly grew much in the same way. It is wonderful to walk with you on this spiritual journey. I am so happy that we found each other again. You are patient and always listen when I have my next great idea. Whether I finish it right away, later down the road, or never you constantly support me.

I am grateful to all of my unseen Guardians just on the other side. I am able to perceive your assistance and guidance. Sometimes it is a subtle whisper, and other times I need the stronger push into a certain direction. Thank you to all who are assisting me with your messages, guidance, love, and grace so needed during these times.

Notes

About The Author

Dr. Jane E. Rackley is a Chiropractic Physician who has been in private practice for over 18 years. She has offered many cutting-edge treatments for her patients throughout the years including Chiropractic, Clinical Nutrition, Transformational Weight Management™, Frequency Specific Microcurrent, and BioEnergetic Medicine. As a Healer, she is dedicated to bringing the greatest level of health and well-being into as many lives as possible. For over 16 years, she has been graced with the direct teachings of a living Spiritual Master in her life. She regularly practices and teaches these core spiritual concepts helping to direct others how to heal. She currently works in her private practice located in Fort Wayne, Indiana.

She also facilitates various Transformational Workshops, retreats, and classes. Her website: www.DrJaneRackley.com

Books By The Author

Love Yourself and Be Healed: Awakening © October 2014.

Transformational Workbook: *Love Yourself and Be Healed: Awakening* © February 2017